unlock your
dog's
potential

unlock your
dog's
potential

How to achieve a calm and happy canine

Sarah Fisher

D&C

David and Charles

For Robyn Hood, a unique and inspiring teacher and friend whose humour, support and advice is so greatly appreciated.

A DAVID & CHARLES BOOK
Copyright © David & Charles Limited 2007

David & Charles is an F+W Publications Inc. company
4700 East Galbraith Road
Cincinnati, OH 45236

First published in the UK in 2007

Copyright © Sarah Fisher 2007

Sarah Fisher has asserted her right to be identified as author of this work in accordance with the Copyright, Designs and Patents Act, 1988.

A catalogue record for this book is available from the British Library.

ISBN-13: 978-0-7153-2638-1
ISBN-10: 0-7153-2638-4

Printed in the People's Republic of China by SNP-Leefung
for David & Charles
Brunel House, Newton Abbot, Devon

Commissioning Editor: Jane Trollope
Assistant Editor: Louise Clark
Project Editor: Jo Weeks
Art Editor: Marieclare Mayne
Production Controller: Kelly Smith

Photography: Bob Atkins

Page 30 courtesy of F.D. Vargen and page 122 courtesy of KT.

Visit our website at www.davidandcharles.co.uk

David & Charles books are available from all good bookshops; alternatively you can contact our Orderline on 0870 9908222 or write to us at FREEPOST EX2 110, D&C Direct, Newton Abbot, TQ12 4ZZ (no stamp required UK only); US customers call 800-289-0963 and Canadian customers call 800-840-5220.

Sarah Fisher is the UK's highest qualified Equine and Companion Animal Instructor. She trained with Linda Tellington Jones and Robyn Hood and now runs the UK office for TTEAM & TTouch International. Sarah makes regular TV appearances in the UK, writes for national magazines and also teaches one- and two-day workshops.

CONTENTS

FOREWORD

I wish every dog owner could meet Sarah Fisher. As this is, unfortunately, never going to happen, she's done the next best thing and written a book about dogs as she sees them. I've been on at her for years to do it, and she's finally documented her ideas, which are readable, radical and compassionate in the extreme. I particularly love reading her case reports, which reveal how she has transformed animals that are beyond ordinary rehabilitation techniques.

Assessing behaviour, body tension and pain patterns is difficult. Doing something creative about them can be daunting. In almost imperceptible steps, Sarah's work bridges the gap between being just a passive dog owner to becoming an observant, understanding, pro-active dog guardian. By reading this book you could take this journey with your dog.

In a hundred years from now, I'm convinced that people will look back on this sort of book as we do now on the work of early social reformers. They had compassion where previously there was none. They sought to understand the downtrodden. They spoke up for the disenfranchised, urging more fortunate people to honour and respect them as fellow beings. Sarah does this for our animal companions.

Sarah is pioneering a new awareness of our dogs' subtle intelligence, both of mind and body. By opening the eyes of dog owners she is rekindling a dialogue that dogs began with us thousands of years ago, when they first cautiously stepped out of the forest to take their place by the prehistoric human fire. As she says in the book – 'A mind that has been expanded by new experiences cannot go back to its old dimensions.'

This book will save lives – human and canine. It is an incredible distillation of Sarah's unique ability to perceive and understand dogs. If you can glean even a morsel of what she is saying, you and your dog will be greatly enriched.

Nick Thompson BSc (Hons), BVMBS, VetMFHom, MRCVS

IMPROVE YOUR DOG'S LIFE

Sharing our lives with a dog should be an enriching and rewarding experience. For the majority of trainers and owners, the harmonious relationship they have with their canine companions is based on co-operation, appreciation, trust and loyalty. If you already enjoy this sort of bond, you can further enhance the partnership by working through this book, which will give you a greater awareness and a deeper understanding of your dog. You can use the information provided to help him lead a longer, happier and healthier life by improving his sense of wellbeing and by reducing unwanted behaviours such as leash pulling, spinning, hyperactivity, excessive barking, chewing and so on, while also deepening the rapport between you.

The book guides you through kind, gentle and effective techniques to enable your dog to overcome any specific concerns he may have, such as fear of the vet, timidity, noise sensitivity, noise phobias, including fear of thunder and fireworks, separation anxiety, or issues around grooming or toe nail trimming. Using these techniques in conjunction with appropriate veterinary care can help your dog cope more easily with niggling health concerns such as arthritis, hip displasia or spondylosis or enable him to recover more quickly from injury, disease or surgery. You can also reduce the effects that old age has upon his body. The book explains how, by studying your dog's coat pattern and posture, you can spot physical and emotional changes more quickly and take the necessary steps to prevent them from becoming a problem in the future.

Different challenges

If you are struggling to cope with a dog that is in your care you can reduce unwanted behaviours and establish a unique relationship with him using these proven methods. They will also help you to teach him how to respond to situations instead of simply reacting to them.

If you work with a variety of dogs, such as in a shelter or in any training capacity including service dogs, you can use the observations to assess the temperament and suitability of the dog for a particular lifestyle. By learning some of the simple TTouches and groundwork exercises you can improve a dog's focus and therefore his ability to be trained. You can help a dog realize his full potential whatever the goal, and increase a shelter dog's chances of being re-homed.

Whatever your reasons for reading this book – one thing is certain. You will never look at a dog in the same way again.

Battersea Dogs and Cats Home

The employees and canine residents of Battersea Dogs and Cats Home feature regularly in this book. Battersea is one of the most famous animal shelters in the UK. It was founded in 1860 by Mrs Mary Tealby to care for London's lost and abandoned dogs, and in 1883 opened its doors to cats in need of help. The home continues to care for stray and unwanted animals at its three centres in Battersea (South London), Brands Hatch and Old Windsor. Since it opened, Battersea has taken in over three million cats and dogs.

Battersea's aims are to Rescue, Reunite, Rehabilitate, Rehome. Many of the dogs that find their way to Battersea are true strays and are successfully reunited with their owners. Others have been abandoned or are handed in to the home because their owners are unable (or unwilling) to care for them any more. In 2004 alone Battersea found new homes for 5,814 animals. As well as providing full-time care, including on-site veterinary support, Battersea also runs a dedicated rehabilitation unit for dogs with behavioural issues, to increase their chances of finding a new home.

The Tellington TTouch

It was my partner Tony Head who first came across the work of Linda Tellington Jones while he was in Los Angeles. When he called me to tell me about an extraordinary technique that helped dogs overcome health and behavioural issues using gentle exercises, which he had seen on the television, I laughed. In fact, I teased him for being suckered into a well-made infomercial. However, what I didn't realize was that this one demonstrated how Linda's approach could illicit profound changes in even the most difficult dogs.

A couple of months later I picked up a book entitled *The Tellington Touch* at an animal health seminar. I flipped through the pages and I was hooked. Coming from a human health background and with a passion for Traditional Chinese medicine, Linda's explanation of her work made total sense to me. I didn't realize at the time that this was the same technique I had dismissed only a few weeks earlier. I met Linda when she visited the UK and within four days had flown out to Wyoming to attend a Tellington TTouch horse course at the beautiful Bitteroot Ranch. Now it was Tony who was laughing.

Although I initially qualified as an Equine Practitioner in America, it wasn't long before I was travelling between home and the US again to work with Linda and Robyn Hood on the companion courses.

Training in Tellington TTouch techniques has transformed my life. For over a decade I have had the privilege and pleasure of working with some extraordinary people, and I travel around the UK and abroad giving seminars and teaching private clients, shelter staff and members of the public everything that I have had the great fortune to learn.

Working with a wide variety of animals, in different cultures and in particular with a diverse mix of dog breeds has been invaluable. Though the presenting problems may vary in each situation, their origins are usually the same – stress, tension, confusion, and/or fear. Every animal that I have worked with has also been linked by the aspirations of their owners and carers. All share a mutual desire to help each being become the most successful they can be by using kind, effective methods.

TTouch cannot save every dog. It cannot remove every possible trace of worry from an animal's life, nor offer a guarantee that the destructive, reactive, 'please-let-me slaughter-that-cat' hooligan who has graced your life will become a permanently laidback, couch potato whose new goal is to raise orphaned kittens. What it can do, however, is reduce stress all round, improve the dog's levels of self-confidence and self-control, and offer him an alternative way of

In addition to the bodywork, TTouch uses a unique system of groundwork

t was my partner Tony Head who first discovered the work developed by Linda Tellington Jones

showing his concern when in a worrying situation. Most importantly it shows the owner or handler an exciting, unique, rewarding and highly successful way of helping their dog and enables them to develop a greater understanding and deeper appreciation of their canine companion and his anxieties.

UNDERSTAND THE BASICS

The aim of this section is to give you some basic and simplified information on the nervous system, balance, proprioception, and a dog's responses, sensory integration and pain memory. It is not vital to know any of this in order to work with your dog but it will help you to understand why groundwork and bodywork are so effective in improving posture, performance and behaviour.

Physical balance and…

The relationship between physical and behavioural problems

There is usually a reason for unwanted behaviour, and even extreme patterns of behaviour in dogs can often be attributed to underlying physical causes or are accompanied by areas of tension held in the dog's body. For example, a dog that has tension through the hindquarters and that habitually holds his tail between his legs is likely to be noise-sensitive, nervous of new situations and wary of strangers. He may also be concerned about travelling in a car. When tension in the hindquarters is reduced, the associated behaviours diminish.

While breed type, genetics, lack of training, inappropriate management, poor diet, lack of socialization, and so on can be contributory factors to some unwanted behaviours, the influence that posture has on the way a dog thinks, feels and learns cannot be overlooked. Many of the anti-social behaviours that develop in dogs may also stem from frustration and stress, but these too have an adverse effect on the posture of the dog. A dog that is under duress because his need to perform instinctive behaviours, such as herding for example, is not being satisfied is likely to carry tension through his neck, shoulders and back. This posture in turn triggers higher arousal and more reactive behaviours.

The exercises described in this book (see 'Taking steps to help your dog', p.74) can play an invaluable role in rehabilitating even the most challenging of dogs. In humans, slow movement and touch can help

…emotional balance are linked

Sally carries tension around her tail and hindquarters…

…She is noise-sensitive and worried about travelling in a car

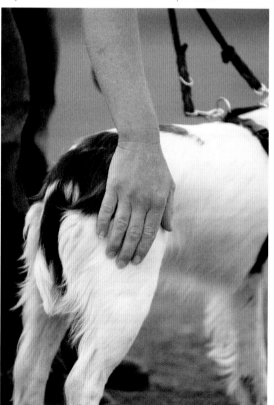

to increase the neurotransmitters responsible for the feel-good factor, which include dopamine and serotonin. It is, therefore, likely that the TTouch bodywork and groundwork exercises bring the same benefits to dogs. When these techniques are used with dogs that are over the top or nervous, they settle and become more relaxed in a surprisingly short space of time. They become more considered and less automatic in their responses. This approach also has the added bonus of promoting a sense of calm in the person using the techniques, which is important when working with any dog.

Behaviour and emotional and mental wellbeing are, therefore, closely linked to a dog's physical state, and each can affect the other for better or worse. Changing an undesirable posture to a more functional one not only relieves physical discomfort and reduces stress but also encourages more efficient body and brain use. A dog that is moving in a considered and balanced way is generally less reactive than a dog that is stiff and rigid. A dog that is calm, contented and supple through his body is less prone to injury and is more likely to stay healthy as stress undermines the immune system. He can process new information faster, is easier to train, and is generally more reliable in his behaviour and performance. In addition, a dog that is happy to be handled in every part of his body will be less concerned by visits to the vet (see also p.35) and the groomer and will be able to adapt more readily to new situations. He will be more social, more confident and will recover more quickly if something does upset or concern him.

Gemma is extremely nervous about hand contact and bites if touched

Fake hands (see p.31) and different tools, such as a paintbrush, change a dog's expectation of human contact and give them a new experience, enabling them to move beyond their habitual responses

What are bodywork and groundwork?

- Bodywork consists of specific, passive movements of the skin, legs, tail and ears to increase circulation and release tension.
- Groundwork consists of slow, considered exercises on the leash over patterns of poles, through cones and over different surfaces to improve co-ordination and balance.

The nervous system

The nervous system detects and interprets changes in conditions both inside and outside the body and responds to them accordingly (see diagram). It works with the endocrine system but is faster in its reactions. It carries sensory input to the processing centres in the brain and spinal cord, interprets the information and then transmits it to effector cells, such as the muscles, which move in response.

Balance and proprioception

Balance is a state of body equilibrium or stability where the dog is distributing his weight equally on all four feet and is able to move and alter his posture as required without the need for obvious re-organization of his body.

Self-confidence and self-control influence – and are influenced by – self-carriage. A dog that is physically out of balance will tend to be more reactive and more emotional than a dog that is evenly developed through the body.

Proprioception is the part of the nervous system that gives your dog conscious awareness of the positions of his joints without him having to look at them. It is also part of the dog's co-ordination system. Dogs with poor proprioception and poor balance may be perceived as being over the top, hyperactive, clingy or clumsy. They may leap in the air, spin or pull when on the leash, knock things over, run into their handler and

Nervous system

The nervous system is divided into two main parts: the central nervous system and the peripheral nervous system.

Central nervous system

- Consists of the brain and spinal cord.
- Receives input from the sense organs such as the ears, eyes and skin, and sends signals to the muscles and glands via the peripheral nervous system.

Peripheral nervous system

- Largely made up of nerves connecting the brain and spinal cord to the rest of the body.
- Undertakes complex tasks through a vast communicating network of nerves and ganglia.
- Has two important divisions: the autonomic nervous system and the somatic nervous system.

Somatic nervous system

- Controls the muscles for voluntary or conscious movement.

Autonomic nervous system

- Concerned with the unconscious regulation of internal body functioning.
- Consists of two sets of nerve cells that have opposite effects on the body: the parasympathetic system and the sympathetic system.

Parasympathetic nervous system

- Conserves energy in the body, decreasing heart and respiration rates, promoting relaxation, activating the digestive system, dilating blood vessels and so on.

Sympathetic nervous system

- Prepares the body for exertion, including flight, by tightening muscles, raising heart and respiration rates, slowing gut function, constricting blood vessels and so on.

Dogs with poor balance are often clingy…

…They may also find it hard to walk calmly on a lead

even fall over. They may find it particularly hard to travel in the car and may have real concerns about walking through doorways or narrow spaces.

Fear and pain and pain memory

When they first occur, injuries obviously cause acute pain and affect movement, but even after the injury has healed the dog may behave as though there is still discomfort in the area. This may be due to the fact that the dog altered his way of moving and standing to compensate for the original injury and has developed an uneven posture, or it may be that he has an expectation or memory of pain. Pain memory is a well-known phenomenon and has been researched in the human field. It means that, for example, a dog may still be sensitive about having his leg handled even though the actual injury to the ligament or bone has healed. He may anticipate pain from the collar or from being groomed, even if the cause of the initial problem has been addressed. Pain memory can be frustrating and can cause confusion since it may be difficult to know whether or not the original problem still exists.

Fear and pain can trigger similar responses and it is important to recognize that, whatever the cause, the concern is still very real for the dog. Bodywork and ground exercises can help to change learned responses by influencing the nervous system and improving sensory integration. If pain memory or fear of pain is the issue, a difference in the dog's behaviour should be noticeable soon after work begins.

Ra was the subject of a cruelty and neglect case. He had a deformed spine and was extremely stressed around people. A half body wrap (p.93) was used to help him overcome his fear of contact and within a very short space of time he was enjoying being TTouched by two people

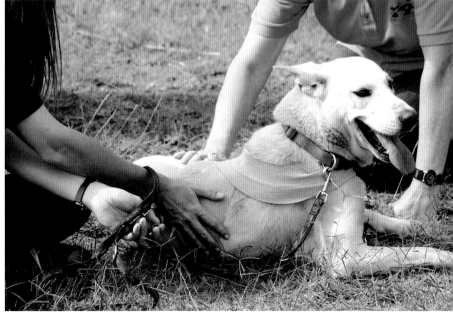

Sensory integration

The senses work together, and sensory experiences include touch, movement, sight, sound, pull of gravity, smell, taste and body awareness. The process by which the nervous system organizes and interprets this information is called sensory integration. It provides an important foundation for learning and behaviour.

Studies of children with poor sensory integration show that they can lack self-awareness, self-control, focus and the ability to self-calm. They may also have difficulty in adapting to new situations, be clumsy, have poor socialization skills and may over- or under-react to containment, touch, movement, sight or sound. Many dogs that have behavioural issues or those that are deemed to be hard to train and over the top, exhibit some, if not all of the above symptoms. They may have a short concentration span, they may be over-stimulated by touch, sound or movement and they will often lack the ability to self-calm.

Bodywork and groundwork help to improve sensory integration. Both are valuable tools in reducing unwanted behaviours without the need to resort to dominance, fear or force, which can trigger more stress responses. Incorporating specific exercises or techniques that improve sensory integration when working with dogs, such as putting a T-shirt or half body wrap on the dog (see p.93) or teaching him to use a low-level teeter totter (see saw, p.92) or negotiate his way around a labyrinth (see p.118) can dramatically improve a dog's behaviour in a relatively short space of time.

Narrow eyes and folded ears may indicate that the dog is becoming concerned or feels threatened

Digging…

…and reluctance to move can be a sign that the dog is confused, nervous or unsure

Body language and communication

It is important to recognize how a dog shows distress or concern. The more obvious language of the dog such as growling, whining, barking or nipping is well known, but dogs also have a subtle language that they usually use first. When watching for signs of this, look for a pattern. Dogs, like horses, cats and humans, have some expressions that are very similar whether the dog is relaxing or becoming concerned or stressed. The way to differentiate between the two is to look at the speed and frequency with which the behaviour is occurring, as well as considering the situation as a whole. For example a wagging tail is primarily thought of as being a sign of a happy dog. In fact it can also mean that the dog is agitated or aroused.

Pay attention to the eyes. A hardening, widening or pinching of the eye or wrinkling of the lids around the eyes can be a good indicator that the dog is uncomfortable or concerned, and the eyes are often one of the first things to change in these circumstances. These responses are usually accompanied by a tightening around the base of the ear and a tensing of the muscles around the muzzle and over the head. The breath will become shallow or the dog may even seem as though he is holding his breath. The head may either lift or lower, accompanied by bracing through the neck and back. Some dogs shut down, with the eye appearing dull and disinterested.

The set of the ear is another indicator of a dog's state of mind. Look for small movements as well as the more obvious. A calm dog will have a relaxed ear while a nervous dog will have a folded, flat or pinned ear. An aroused dog or a dog that is in a constant state of alertness will have ears that are tight and carried forward.

Reluctance to move, rushing, chewing or licking the same part of the body, digging, turning the hindquarters, turning the head, walking away or lifting a front leg, can also be signs that the dog is unsure or concerned.

Dogs also use their body language to communicate with each other – to calm down an exuberant dog or to let another dog know that they are friendly, for example. Some dogs are more adept at this than others but even dogs with poor communication skills can learn how to 'talk' appropriately to other dogs and people.

Concerned or relaxed?

Some signs of concern	Some signs of relaxation
Frequent shallow sighing	Slow sighing
Gulping	Deep regular breathing
Yawning	Slow yawning
Fast lip licking	Slow lip licking
Mouthing	Relaxed neck and back
Scratching	Stretching
Clamped jaw	Relaxed muzzle and lip
Elevated heart rate	Soft eye

Hard, glazed eyes, tension across the forehead and around the base of the ears can be a sign of stress

Softening of the eyes, forehead, and ears along with slow lip licking is a sign that the dog is beginning to relax

Dogs use their body language to communicate with each other. These dogs (top and above) are meeting for the first time and are friendly and polite in their approach

'Shouting'

Most people who work with dogs will have heard a description of a dog-biting incident, where there was apparently no warning that the bite was about to occur. In fact, this is highly unlikely to be the case. In many instances the dog would have given a series of signals to communicate that he was feeling threatened, unsure or was trying to diffuse a situation but these signals were probably being overlooked or misinterpreted by the person interacting with the dog, due to their lack of awareness. If the more subtle signals go unnoticed, the dog

will probably become more desperate to communicate his anxiety as his stress levels continue to rise. His language will become louder as a result. Once a dog has learned that 'shouting' is the only way he will be heard, he is likely to continue in the same vein.

Volatile responses can become as entrenched as the postural habits described later (pp.40–73). The dog may lose confidence in his ability to communicate in a more socially acceptable manner and may be labelled as a dominant, alpha, aggressive dog that needs putting firmly back in his place. In some cases he may have been

The five Fs

The dog has five reactions to stimuli which will tell you that he is struggling with the situation or is alarmed. They will often be preceded by the more subtle signals (see 'Shouting', above) but can also happen so quickly that the smaller changes may go unnoticed.

- **FLIGHT**

This is generally the first instinctive response since it makes more sense to flee from a perceived threat than risk possible injury or even death. The senses become heightened. The heart rate rises and the blood supply to the extremities is inhibited to allow increased blood flow to the major muscle groups, heart and lungs to facilitate a speedy getaway.

- **FIGHT**

The flight/fight reflexes are closely linked. Fight usually kicks in when the option to flee is prevented. Dogs are, therefore, often more reactive when on a lead or when they feel trapped. Aggression in dogs can arise from frustration, stress, panic, inappropriate handling, poor breeding, poor nutrition and lack of socialization. It can also stem from fear, with the dog quickly learning – sometimes from a single experience – that attack is the best form of defence. It can also be triggered by a reaction to drugs, pain or other medical problems, which must be addressed.

- **'FREEZE'**

This response usually occurs when a dog is frightened, feels threatened or is unsure. The dog stands still, has a hard or fixed look in his eye, is rigid through his body, and may look as though he is holding his breath.

The dog's stillness might be misinterpreted as him being calm and enjoying the attention/situation, or that he is refusing to move because he is stubborn and doesn't want to get into the car, walk down the road, move away.

Biting, rushing, leaping and spinning, leash grabbing and

so on when the dog does move are all validations that the dog was rooted because he was actually in 'freeze'. If you see any dog go into freeze, stop what you are doing or are asking him to do immediately. Go back a few steps to something he found easy or give him a break. This will help him grow in confidence and he will trust you more.

Dogs can freeze for a split second before biting. This may not always give someone enough time to get out the way but there are usually other signs of stress that will precede the actual freeze (see 'Concerned or relaxed?', p.17). When the dog is with a handler/owner and you are working together or you are near the dog, if freeze occurs, ask the handler to move the dog away from you quickly but calmly. If you are the one to step back, your movement is more likely to trigger a bite.

- **'FAINT'**

This response is rare and cannot always be described as a true faint although dogs with certain medical problems can quite literally pass out. If this happens the dog must be taken to a vet immediately. In the context of the five responses to stimuli, 'faint' is used to describe a situation where the dog is totally overloaded, shuts down and drops to the ground. This behaviour is seen more in horses but it can also occur in dogs if they are repeatedly punished or are stressed to the extreme. No animal should ever be pushed to this point.

- **FOOL AROUND** (ALSO REFERRED TO AS **FIDGET** OR **FIDDLE**)

This very common response is often misinterpreted as boredom, hyperactivity, or that the dog is trying to gain control of a situation. The dog may rush about, leap in the air, grab the leash, mouth the handler, or become rough and over the top when playing a game. Fool around can also be misinterpreted as the dog enjoying himself. This may encourage the handler to escalate his or her own behaviour, which can alarm the dog further.

trained or encouraged to behave in a reactive way. Whatever the reason, as far as he is concerned, his behaviour is wholly appropriate.

Punishment is not the answer

Punishing a dog for giving warning signs such as growling can lead to further problems. If you think about it from the dog's point of view he is being told off for communicating in this manner when he feels threatened or unsure. If the reason for the concern is not addressed and the owner or handler continues down the punishment route the dog will do exactly what he is being asked to do. He will stop growling. And probably go straight for a bite next time he is exposed to the threat or is concerned.

Dog body language is fascinating. Norwegian dog trainer Turid Rugaas has studied this subject for over a decade. Her book *On Talking Terms with Dogs: Calming Signals* is a must for any dog owner or trainer. An understanding and awareness of 'calming signals' can help you to recognize the early triggers for unwanted behaviours and enable you to take steps to reduce a dog's anxiety before it escalates.

Freeze is often misinterpreted. It can be a sign of concern

The dog may engage in a displacement activity, such as sniffing, licking or fidgeting about, if he is unsure about a situation but is unable to remove himself from the stimulus. Punishing the dog or forcefully stopping him from expressing himself like this can trigger another response such as fight.

Young dogs in particular have a short concentration span. They may go into 'fool around' when they have reached the limits of their capacity for learning. If the dog does go into fool around, look at his behaviour in the context in which it occurs and stop what you are doing or asking him to do. Give him a complete break, reduce his stress levels by doing some bodywork, or walk him slowly and calmly, making a curving, S-shaped path. The behaviour usually subsides once the trigger has been removed.

Labelling of dogs

Humans tend to like to label behaviours or problems. Sometimes this is to the detriment of the dog as we may inadvertently misinterpret his actions. Once a label is placed on a dog it can be extremely difficult to remove it. Labelling may not only limit our ability to help the dog but might actually exacerbate the situation. Take a dog that has issues over food for example. If the behaviour is referred to as 'food aggression', it immediately conjures up a rather bleak and threatening image. If, however, the dog is described as having 'irritable bowl syndrome', it changes the way the owner or handler views the problem. It also describes the situation more appropriately, since dogs can develop unwanted behaviours around food for several reasons:

- They may have been deliberately starved or underfed
- They may have been teased with food

- They may have had to fight for food in order to survive
- They may have been taken away too early from their mother
- They may have a nutritional deficiency so never feel satisfied after eating
- They may have a gut imbalance, a dental problem or a food allergy that makes eating an uncomfortable experience
- They may have been punished for stealing or begging for food instead of being trained appropriately
- Food may be or may have become a really high-value resource in their life due to boredom and/or frustration.

The position of the food bowl and/or the room where the dog eats may also be part of the problem. If the bowl is against the wall for example and the dog has tension through his hindquarters, he may be unable to relax when eating as movement behind him may be a cause for concern.

Dogs are social animals and with appropriate handling can interact comfortably with new dogs and new people

It may not always be possible to ascertain when or why the problem started – if you take on a dog from a shelter, for instance – but this doesn't mean the dog will always remain reactive around food. By making changes to the feeding routine, feeding him more frequently, altering the diet, setting up a quiet space where he can eat alone without feeling threatened, and/or reducing stress in general will enable a high proportion of dogs with 'irritable bowl syndrome' to overcome their concerns around food.

The word 'dominant' is another commonly misapplied and inappropriate label. It implies that the dog sees himself as being in charge and suggests that techniques to reduce the ranking of the dog must be imposed to ensure a harmonious existence between man and dog. This approach can make the situation far worse. Dogs are not stupid: they know their carers are people, not dogs. Dogs are social animals that look for and respond to leadership and guidance, just like children. They go through different phases of development as they mature, sometimes changing from one day to the next, and need consistency, positive training and understanding to develop into balanced, confident, self-controlled adults.

When you take a moment to study a dog labelled as 'dominant' and observe his facial expressions, feel the tension patterns (see p.36) through his body and watch how he reacts and responds to stimulus, you will probably start to recognize a dog that is, in fact, insecure, untrained, unsure of his boundaries and in the fight/flight reflex because he is confused, frustrated, or under duress.

Archie's story

When our fantastic and hugely entertaining Battersea dog, Archie, was 18 months old he air-snapped when Tony tried to persuade him to move from the sofa. As any Lurcher owner knows, the sofa is a very important resource in a sight-hound's life, so Archie's behaviour could have been misinterpreted as bed-guarding. It could also have

Archie has matured into a gentle and fantastic dog

Tony and Archie

been misinterpreted as pure dominant behaviour. Archie might have been refusing to do as Tony asked because the dog perceived himself as ranking higher in the household than Tony, particularly as Tony spends a significant amount of time working away from home. The second train of thought could have been backed up further with the added knowledge that Archie was a shelter dog who had been found as a London stray with a catalogue of behaviours that we had to work through – when we adopted him at six months old he was:

- Highly stressed
- Noise-sensitive to the point of phobia
- Very nervous of people, with a particular concern about men
- Hysterical when in a car
- Totally over the top with a tendency to nip when over-excited
- Highly adept at making up his own entertainment
- The BIGGEST thief that ever walked the planet on four paws
- And Chief Destroyer of All Beautiful Things – including my Anya Hindmarch handbag (although to be totally fair he didn't exactly destroy it, it was more of an unfortunate snapping of a handle that occurred as he legged it from our house with the handbag swinging from his neck, well and truly ensnared by his glorious pointy features while truffling through the contents of the bag).

Reading through this list it would be easy to believe that there was the potential for other behavioural problems to develop as he matured. Fortunately for Archie, Tony and I both know that this type of behaviour often has other roots.

I had been upstairs at the time of the incident and when Tony came running into our room to tell me what had happened my first words were: 'Oh No! What happened to him today?'

Tony thought back and remembered that Jet, the German Shepherd who lived at our farm, had jumped on Archie earlier that day when they were out running in the fields. I shot downstairs and sat with Archie on the sofa to check him over. Sure enough there were signs of an injury. The hair in the middle of his back was standing up and the soft tissue on either side of the spine was swollen and hot. His eyes were hard and staring and he looked hunched up, highly uncomfortable and concerned. When I asked him to get up in his own time, the movement was very slow and laboured.

This was one of the many situations that I have been in with an animal where I am so grateful to know about TTouch. I did light Clouded Leopard TTouches and Lifts (see p.95) all over Archie's body, and worked his ears. Within 10 minutes he was much calmer and more relaxed. He was referred for McTimoney treatment (see box, below, right) and this together with TTouch work helped him make a full recovery. Although he may always have a vulnerable area in his back, I can keep him happy and mobile and can spot the moment he needs further treatment by watching his coat and checking the mobility of his skin.

I have worked with several dogs that are labelled as bed-guarders and in a high proportion of them there has been some significant amount of sensitivity through the back and/or hindquarters.

If you think about this logically, it makes sense that a dog that is uncomfortable would put up some protest when asked to move from his place of rest. Not only may it be difficult for him to get up because any movement is hard but he may have also stiffened up more while lying down. If the dog is punished for this behaviour, the trigger for his concern will change. It won't be the actual act of moving that now causes the anxiety but the fear of a person approaching. His anxiety levels will rise as soon as a person walks into the room.

If your dog grumbles when you approach his bed, watch how he moves on and off the lead. Note whether he is stiffer after a long walk or rigorous exercise. You may not notice a change in his movement until he has slept for a while, or even until the following day. If you drive to your local park or woods to walk your dog, note whether he is hesitant to get out of the car when you get back home as this can be also be a sign that he is uncomfortable after exercise. Dragging any dog from his place of rest can trigger a bite. Positive training methods offer both a motive and reward. They will not escalate a dog's concerns and are kind, safe and effective.

Dogs can make fantastic companions for children, provided both are taught how to interact with each other in an appropriate way

Maisie learned how to use TTouch from an early age. She has an excellent rapport with all animals as a result

Children and dogs

The labelling of dogs or misunderstanding of a dog's language and responses can be particularly worrying when it comes to the interaction between children and dogs. Dogs make fantastic companions for children but things can quickly get out of hand if warning signs that the dog is concerned are ignored. Showing children how to clicker train (see p.26) their dog can help to develop a wonderful bond and teaches them how to achieve a sit, recall, stay and so on without giving conflicting signals or leaning over the dog to push it into the sit or down.

TTouch helps to teach a child how to handle and engage with the puppy or dog in an appropriate way and gives the whole family skills to quieten an over-exuberant dog without escalating the behaviour by a mistake or misinterpreting it as a game. It is particularly important that children learn how to behave around dogs, as many dogs are nervous or overly aroused by children's noisy activities and erratic approach. Never take any risks with dogs where the safety of a child might be compromised.

McTimoney chiropractic

The McTimoney approach to chiropractic is based on a holistic assessment of the individual, including wellbeing and quality of life. McTimoney uses speed and light force to toggle the vertebrae into the correct position and to make other adjustments where necessary, such as to the sacrum, pelvis and cranium. The aim of a McTimoney chiropractor is to stimulate the body's ability to self-heal, a concept that blends perfectly with TTouch philosophy. As such, McTimoney chiropractic has become an integral part of my work.

Jenna

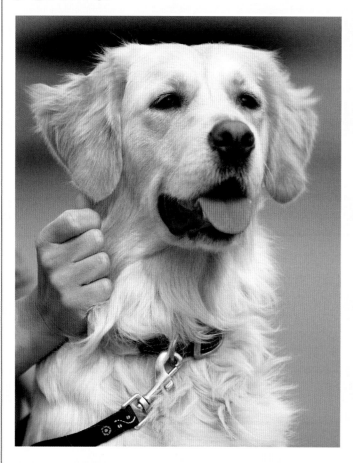

Anna came to our farm to find ways to help Jenna, her two-year-old Golden Retriever, quieten and settle in the home. She was also concerned about the relationship between Jenna and her son, Ben. Someone had suggested that Jenna was reactive towards Ben because the dog saw herself as ranking higher in the household than Ben. This attitude is alarming because it implies that the child must be assertive with the dog, which can have disastrous repercussions for both dog and child.

Anna told me that Ben has some learning difficulties, finds it hard to focus and had been rough with Jenna at times. When a dog feels threatened, they have to warn the child or person away. If their concerns are ignored and appropriate steps are not taken quickly to change the situation, the dog's behaviour will become more volatile. Anna had tried to explain this to Ben but a young child may be unable to grasp the concept of the possible consequences of their actions. They cannot always understand something they have not experienced and no child should have the knowledge of what a dog bite feels like in order to learn appropriate behaviour with their pet.

Anna takes up the story

Various members of my family have owned dogs as pets and both my grandfather (who bred Dachshunds) and my mother (who owned Red Setters) had had issues with training. Therefore, when the time came for me as a young adult to own my own dog, I approached training with some trepidation.

My first dog, a black Labrador, had a wonderful disposition and was extremely bright, so picked up the basic obedience commands very quickly, although she was terrible on the lead and at coming when called. She was also easy to house train. I guess things were simpler then, as my son Ben (now seven and a half years old) was only four months old when my circumstances dictated I found a new home for her.

Ben and Jenna

Jenna is Ben's dog, and was a gift from me for his sixth birthday. Ben had been asking for a dog for around three years. He had also been pretending to be a dog since he was two years old, 'walking' on all fours, 'barking' at the doorbell, and licking people. I believed that buying him a dog of his own would stop the behaviour, and I was also keen to start teaching him independence and responsibility. He had previously owned smaller animals (fish, guinea pigs and a rabbit), and had dealt well with them.

Within days of Jenna's arrival in our home, it became apparent that even though Ben loved her and enjoyed playing with her,

Tina demonstates TTouch to Anna to show her how she can help Jenna to relax

Children are often erratic in their handling, which can frighten the dog

he was also extremely jealous of the attention that a new puppy demands, and his own dog-like behaviour did not diminish. We attended puppy-training classes as a family, and both Ben and I were taught how to handle and control Jenna. She responded very positively to both of us. However, Ben's behaviour towards Jenna was erratic, to say the least, he would swing between enthusiastic 'bear hugs' around her neck, using her as a pillow, and playing with her, to hitting her, kicking her and (once) throwing a brick at her. Things were coming to a head, and I started considering finding her a new home.

Another of Jenna's habits, which she has picked up from staying at a dog-owning friend's house while we were on holiday, is barking. She not only barks at the doorbell, she barks if someone opens the gate, or if someone walks past on the pavement. This happens day or night, and she takes a while to settle down again. She is also very loud! It was this in particular that was driving me mad (although I was obviously very concerned about Ben and Jenna's relationship too), so I contacted Sarah for some help.

Working with Jenna

Ben and I went to see Sarah at her farm with Jenna, and I told her about Jenna and Ben. Sarah took Ben off separately, while her colleague Tina Constance started work on Jenna. Tina ran her hands over Jenna's body and also watched her walk around. This told her where Jenna was tense, and those spots were then TTouched. You could see Jenna physically relax. It was amazing. Then Sarah came back with Ben, and asked him to take Jenna from me, and follow some simple instructions.

Sarah was rewarding Ben with a clicker (normally used in dog training, see box p.26), and his behaviour with her was incredible. He received a penny for each click he had. Ben also had some dog treats and a clicker to reward Jenna's behaviour. Within a few short minutes he was walking her through a maze, and getting her to jump over a small jump, as well as sitting on command and walking to heel. It proved to him and to me that he is more than capable of treating her nicely, and working with her, and that Jenna is happy to be around him and to obey

Ben learnt how to use a clicker and as he became more focused Jenna, not surprisingly, became more engaged. Ben wore a body wrap so that he could understand how Jenna felt when she was wearing hers

Ben's timing with the clicker was incredible. He formed a wonderful partnership with his dog in a very short space of time

Ben and Jenna worked through all the ground exercises. The session was varied, fun and highly successful

Clicker training

Clicker training is the process of using a small gadget, known as a clicker, to mark the desired behaviour in an animal, such as a dog or a horse. The trainer 'clicks' at the moment the behaviour occurs. The dog is then given a reward, such as a treat, a toy, or even a fuss – whatever is considered of value by the dog – and quickly learns to repeat the behaviour he was doing when he heard the click. Once the dog is confident that the behaviour will get a click and a reward and so consistently repeats the behaviour, a hand signal or voice command can be introduced. The dog learns to watch or listen for the cue/signal, before offering the behaviour that resulted in the click and the reward.

him, as long as she doesn't feel threatened by him. I was shown how to relax Jenna when she becomes nervous or over-excited, by using TTouches around her neck, face, ears and chest. When we went home Ben had 80 pennies, and I had a couple of clickers to continue the training.

Jenna still barks at the doorbell, but it is a work in progress. I have taught my parents the clicker technique to use with Ben, and he is responding just as well with them as he is with me. Jenna is less nervous of Ben now, and Ben is behaving well around her. The best result though is that from his behaviour with Jenna, Ben is earning pocket money at home, as every positive interaction gets a reward. This is a real testament to Sarah and the Tellington TTouch Team!

Puppies

Working with puppies is highly rewarding, and the knowledge that you are helping to shape a dog that will mature into a confident, happy and healthy adult is very satisfying. It is, however, an enormous responsibility and it is important that anyone involved with training youngsters has the ability to spot potential problems before they develop. It is also paramount that owners learn positive training techniques so that their puppy receives clear, consistent signals from all family members, enjoys training both in the home and in class, and learns how to interact with children, adults and other animals. Punishment, pinning an over-exuberant pup to the floor and/or rough handling can create a problem puppy in a matter of weeks.

Marie Miller, a leading TTouch Practitioner and one of the founder members of the UK Association of Pet Dog Trainers says:

'There is a special magic experienced by a family as they welcome their new puppy home. However, it can be very challenging to rear a puppy on through adolescence into adulthood and maintain the excitement of that early relationship. Keeping that magic alive by helping to recognize the early signs of potential problem behaviour and finding kind, fair and effective solutions is hugely rewarding. Those who still expound the theory that our relationship with companion animals is about dominance and submission are extremely unhelpful to the successful development of our puppies. Overbearing, coercive handling and training techniques create an unpleasant and uncomfortable relationship. This can trigger behaviour that is fearful, reactive at one end of the scale, completely shut down at the other and varying degrees in between, depending on the individual puppy.'

Making puppy training sessions varied, fun and rewarding is the key to developing a healthy, happy, balanced dog

Note George's uneven ears. He had tension all down the right side of his neck, even though he was only a few weeks old

This tension made it difficult for him to tolerate contact around his neck and head

Development of habitual postures

Marie also has plenty to say about puppy health:

'Puppies begin to adopt habitual postures early in life. This is governed not only by how they are trained and handled, but also by their individual temperament and the genetic traits developed from selective breeding. Realistically, it doesn't matter why these habitual postures develop, we need only to recognize that they WILL influence the emotional and physical development of the puppy if ignored. TTouch provides valuable and fun tools for both family and puppy to enhance both their relationship and the puppy's awareness of its own body and movement. Bodywork and groundwork can be fitted seamlessly into positive, reward-based training sessions to encourage a posture that helps the puppy to be calm and open to new experiences and life lessons.'

While a healthy pup is generally robust to a degree, its immature frame is highly susceptible to damage. Problems can stem from how puppies are born. If a pup is born backwards, for example, too

TTouch can play an invaluable role in helping puppies overcome concerns about being handled

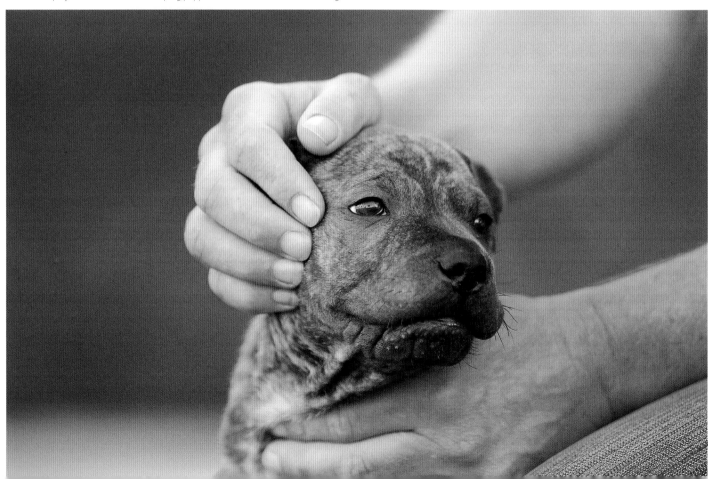

A puppy's neck is very vulnerable. Teaching a puppy to walk on a harness is kinder and safer

much pressure can be applied to the hips and hindquarters during whelping. This may set up long-term issues with the hindquarters and back, which can be linked to behaviours such as noise sensitivity, and other responses associated with the flight/flight reflex. Other injuries can occur once the pup is growing, such as falling out of a high-sided bed or whelping box, being trodden on, kicked or dropped by mistake, tumbling off a piece of furniture or down the stairs. Rough play with siblings or an over-exuberant bitch can also cause problems that may go undetected.

Collars, mouthing and containment

Collars can also cause problems, particularly in the early stages when the puppy is learning to walk on a lead. A puppy's neck is vulnerable and does not have the muscular development of an adult dog. If the puppy is dragged, pulled, flipped over or jarred by a collar, neck and back problems can occur and the puppy may also become collar-shy.

Teaching a puppy to wear a harness is far more beneficial, and if he needs to be removed quickly from a situation for some reason or

runs to the full extent of the lead, a harness ensures there is no risk of causing damage to the neck.

Suckling is important for the development of a healthy dog, physically and emotionally. If a pup is removed too early from his mother and siblings or if the mother dies or rejects the pup he may be slow to mature and may develop unwanted behaviours such as excessive mouthing and chewing and inappropriate play. If you have a puppy that lost contact with his mother too early (under 8 weeks) you can use the TTouches including mouth work (p.98) to help him.

Showing a puppy that containment is both acceptable and enjoyable is a valuable part of handling and training. It also teaches the puppy patience and self-control. This is not the same as restraining a puppy, which can trigger reactive responses.

Puppy owners also have a responsibility to teach the puppy how to interact with other dogs and people without being over the top. Puppies that experience TTouch bodywork and groundwork exercises are generally more advanced, calmer, more appropriate in their behaviour and more balanced on both a physical and emotional level than those that have not had any exposure to these techniques.

Denzil

I met Denzil, a young Rottweiler, while teaching a four-day workshop at Battersea Old Windsor. Although only 10 weeks old, he already had rather extreme behaviours, which were of such concern to Ann O'Brien, Head of Rehab at Battersea Dogs and Cats Home, that he was going to be signed up for euthanasia if he didn't respond to the work.

Denzil was so stressed he was permanently tense around his ears and across the top of his head. He would bite legs, trousers, hands, and arms. He would also snap at faces if picked up. If Den took hold of an article he would growl and really threaten anyone who attempted to remove it from his mouth. Although I have worked successfully with pups like Den before, I was concerned that he was so over the top we might not be able to achieve sufficient changes in his behaviour to help him become content and safe for rehoming.

Working with Denzil

When working with puppies like Denzil it is important to teach the dog that containment is not something to be concerned about. By sitting on the floor with Denzil placed between my knees I could support him gently around the chest. With his head away from me I could avoid the risk of him jumping at my face. As he writhed around, trying to bite my hands and arms I kept my arms and shoulders relaxed and went with his movement as opposed to trying to stop it. Supporting Denzil in this way also meant that I could influence his neck and head position without causing him to panic by forcing contact upon him. I could move the skin on his shoulders with the palms of my hands and introduce light Clouded Leopard TTouches around his chest with my fingers. It is important that any pup has plenty of time out and that the sessions are kept short, so I worked for a few minutes and then let Den explore the room.

Although Den's behaviour quietened a little during the first session, his eyes remained hard, and at times he would go into a complete rage, throwing himself around, growling and snapping. It took a careful balance of using enough groundwork and bodywork with Denzil to change his expectations of what human interaction might mean, while also allowing him time to calm down away from any stimulus.

On the second day of the workshop, I noticed something else that worried me. When he came into the room, Denzil didn't seem to acknowledge anyone that he had met on the first day. I had spent a significant amount of time working with

Rehab dilemma

There are many dogs in the same situation as Denzil and I think it is tragic that pups face destruction at such a young age, but Battersea are realistic in their approach. Some shelters simply do not have the time to work through such difficult problems, often created by the dog's previous owners, albeit by mistake, and are frequently battling against the additional stress that shelter life produces in some dogs.

When weighing up the options, shelters have to look at breed type, the likelihood of finding appropriate homes, the level of the problems that the dog has and the availability of resources that can give the individual dog exactly what he needs for a successful rehabilitation. They also have to justify filling kennel space, potentially long-term, when there are so many dogs waiting to come into shelters that could quickly and easily be rehomed. Shelters also have to consider the levels of stress that the dog is under while in kennels, which may be contributing to the extreme behaviours. Many dogs are destroyed because they cannot cope with the shelter environment. To keep them alive with little chance of finding a home would be cruel, and shelters should not be condemned for facing up to these challenging decisions.

him on the first day but he didn't appear to recognize me at all. There were moments where it seemed as though he was processing the bodywork and groundwork but other times when he still lost the plot.

Making progress

I introduced Denzil to the clicker and also began working with a fake hand (see box, right) to teach him to release toys and objects. Working appropriately with fake hands can be invaluable and this technique provided a major breakthrough with Denzil. He had picked up a ball while we were working in the outside paddock and was growling continuously and threatening anyone who attempted to take it from him. Naturally he responded to the fake hand in the same way while firmly maintaining his hold on the ball. Had I been touching him with my own hand I would have been tempted to stop.

It is important to remember when working through any of this type of behaviour that it is only the human who deems

Using a fake hand

Fake, or false, hands are shaped from rubber and attached to a rigid baton contained within a stuffed shirt sleeve. They are invaluable in working with animals that are hand-shy and for dogs that have a history of biting. They are used to introduce hand contact in a safe, controlled manner and provide an important step in the rehabilitation process.

If you use a fake hand with dogs it is important that you are dextrous and that the false limb becomes a part of you. It has to become an extension of your own arm. The movements must be fluid and calm. Jabbing the dog or making inconsistent and jerky movements with the hand can trigger stress responses and make the situation worse.

A fake hand is a safe way of introducing hand contact to nervous dogs

the behaviour unacceptable or inappropriate. Punishment will therefore only serve to frustrate, confuse or frighten the dog more. As I continued to stroke Den around his muzzle and head with the fake hand, his growling became less intense and his eyes began to soften. When he finally dropped the ball, he was immediately rewarded with a click and a treat. By the end of the day we could touch Den all over, and I could pick him up without any fuss. He had learnt to release toys and had picked up the idea of the clicker with astonishing ease. I was amazed at the intelligence of this little pup and wasn't happy about writing him off just yet.

Fostering Den

However, it wasn't enough for the staff or me to be able to handle Den. He had to learn to respond to other people in a similar way if he was to have any hope of finding a home, so I asked Ann if I could take the puppy to Tilley Farm on foster. Ann knew that I would be realistic but, like me, was keen to explore any option available to him.

When I went back to Battersea to pick up Denzil a week later he greeted me with great gusto, much to my surprise. He behaved impeccably while I clipped on his lead and when I carried him out to my car he was calm and relaxed.

Over the coming weeks Denzil attended a two-day workshop I was teaching at my farm and participated in the week-long practitioner training clinic. He worked with the wonderful Marie Miller who was also was excited by his incredible intelligence,

as was Maria Johnston, another excellent TTouch Practitioner. Maria had her agility bitch Inka at the farm and in the evenings Den and Inka played off lead in the training barn. Inka then taught Den invaluable lessons in how to interact appropriately with another dog. She was fast, playful, gentle but firm and when he became over the top snapping and trying to mount her, she let him know that his behaviour was unacceptable.

My good friend Nick Thompson, a fantastic holistic vet, treated the puppy with homeopathy to help reduce his extreme swings in behaviour, and Denzil never looked back. He learnt to be around horses, and socialized with a wide variety of dogs and people. He was rehomed and lives in a family with two other dogs. He has plenty of walks and swims regularly in the river. I see him frequently and he is maturing into a happy, friendly, outgoing and contented adult.

Denzil has found a perfect home and is now well-socialized, happy and content

Older dogs

Joint stiffness and reduced mobility, impaired hearing, poor balance and poor proprioception are just some of the effects of old age. Memory loss, anxiety and confusion can also affect an aging dog, and bodywork and groundwork can be invaluable in helping to minimize the impact advancing years have upon his mind and body. Nutritional and dietary changes may also be required, and consulting a holistic vet who can support your dog through his later years can help you ensure that your old-age pooch retains a good quality of life to the end.

Shannie feeling the benefits of the TTouch bodywork session

Older dogs often suffer from reduced mobility – Shannie is stiff through her lower back and hindquarters

TTouch work can help older dogs feel more comfortable through the body

Learning some simple acupressure or TTouch techniques will enable you to continue to be an integral part of your dog's health and wellbeing. Even though he may have been retired from service or competitive work, or perhaps can no longer keep up with younger canine household members on long country walks, a few minutes bodywork every day gives you both some valued quiet time together, one on one, that reminds him, if that were needed, that he is and will forever be, incredible, unique and very, very loved.

When the time comes for him to leave your side, TTouch can help you say goodbye. Connecting with a dog in this way during his final moments, or while you are waiting for the vet to arrive, can be a profound and powerful experience. It gives you something positive to do when all else feels beyond control, and brings a little peace and comfort to all involved.

Squidgy is 19 years old. His owner, Adam, gives him a TTouch session every day

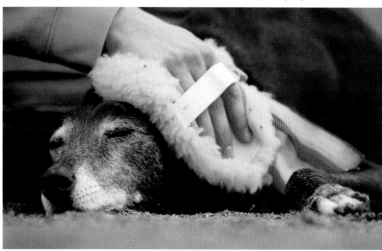

Lucy

In the summer of 1995 an elderly Red Setter was brought to us by the local dog warden. She had been found swimming helplessly around in a nearby river and had not been claimed. We already had a dog, named Christy, and hadn't been thinking about having another, but as soon as I saw that elegant red-coated lady wandering up our drive I knew she'd found a home.

We named her Lucy and despite her advancing years – she was about 14 – she settled quickly, thanks to TTouch. It helped calm her worried pacing in those first few days and reduced the anxiety of the move to a new home so late in life.

Life with Lucy

One of my most vivid memories of Lucy is from her first day in our house. I was sitting on a chair watching her as she slept, smiling at the orang-utan-like form snoozing at my feet and wondering why the fates had brought her to us. As I watched she stirred, rose stiffly and pushed her old grey face into my hands as they lay upon my lap. I reached to gently stroke her ears and was struck by her unmistakable feminine energy – the melting softness of her chestnut coat, her eyes, her muzzle.

Every animal that has touched my life has taught me something. Lucy's presence through some very challenging times served as a constant reminder that it is ways of gentleness that lead to paths of peace, give strength to troubled souls and bring courage to the heart. Despite the hardships of her life Lucy retained a peaceful dignity and a joyous sense of humour that was with her to the end.

Making a decision

I had somehow known from the outset that she would grace our lives for just two years, so I thought I would be ready, but nothing ever prepares you for goodbyes. In 1997, at the end of the summer, Lucy's body began to fail. The gentle movements of TTouch continued to help her ailing body, but on a glorious autumnal day in mid-September, she let me know she'd had enough. Toxins that were building in her body had brought on sudden fits, and as I watched her aimless plodding around the garden, blindly stumbling over Christy gnawing quietly on a bone I knew that it was time. I put a half body wrap on Lucy to help her balance and went inside to make the call.

Making a decision

At last, and all too soon, the vet arrived. Lucy went straight to meet him, now strangely focused and alert. She turned to look at Christy, shot back across the lawn and grabbed the bone. Then, with head held high, she trotted back into the house and stood, tail wagging, in the hall. The vet thought this would make it harder for me to let her go but in a way it made it easier. It brought a fleeting respite from the sadness, and still brings a smile. As I stood by her, Lucy dropped the bone and wandered, vacant-eyed again, into the garden for the last time. We followed her and as the vet sat on the bench she came to him and raised her paw. I hugged her tight, ran my hands over her body and told her that I loved her. I could feel the rattling of her heart against my arm as I held her still, stroked her ears to keep her calm and did soft Clouded Leopard TTouches around her neck and shoulder to relax her. She never flinched as the needle slid under her wrinkled skin and as I felt the life slip from her, my tears fell to kiss the noble dome of her dear, old head.

Letting go

There can be nothing worse than standing, helpless, as a beloved pet nears death. TTouch enables you to help them and say goodbye in a way that is special and unique. It allows a lifetime of love to pass through your hands in a single moment.

If you are struggling to come to terms with the loss of a dog or if you were unable to be with him at the time of death, take a few quiet moments and connect with him once more. Imagine sending gentle TTouches to your pet, run your fingers through their coat. Tell them everything that was left unsaid. I have had enough experiences of death to know they will hear you.

TTouch techniques in veterinary practice

TTouch has useful applications in a veterinary practice, and both vets and veterinary assistants benefit from qualifying as TTouch practitioners to help them in their work.

• Ear work

As well as preventing or reducing shock, ear work (p.103) can help to calm a distressed or anxious dog before, during and after examination. It is also extremely helpful for dogs that are fretful when they are coming round from sedation. In addition it helps to warm up a cold dog and is easily taught to owners so that they can help their dog once he goes home.

There is a shock point at the end of the ear – doing circular TTouches with your thumb on this site is very relaxing and can help settle a nervous dog

• Mouth work

Being able to apply mouth work (p.98) is extremely helpful for those who are treating dogs that are reluctant to eat. I have many testimonials from veterinary nurses who were astounded to see their charges diving into a bowl of food after a few minutes of mouth work. It also helps to reassure a nervous, vocal dog.

• Clouded Leopard

A few of these TTouches (p.96) around the shoulders and scruff can settle a dog before he is injected or microchipped. They can also be used as an apology after the event. When used around the base of the tail and hindquarters, they prepare a dog for having his temperature taken.

• Balance Leash or Balance Leash Plus

Veterinarians often also find TTouch leading techniques helpful in their work. These simple leading techniques (see pp.82–89) can be used when the dog is being reunited with his owner following a stay at the clinic or when leaving the consulting room. It helps to keep the dog in balance and reduces tension on the neck while he is making a hasty exit from the practice.

• Towel or sling

This is a far less stressful way of taking a reluctant or hesitant dog through to the kennels or into the waiting room than dragging him by his collar.

Use a towel or a sling to walk a reluctant dog into kennels or into the surgery

• Half body wrap

Popping a half body wrap (p.93) or a T-shirt on the dog before he goes into the veterinary practice can help him feel more secure. It can also help to reduce his anxiety about toe nail clipping or having his temperature taken. For a vet examination, the wrap is more suitable as it gives better access to the body.

If your dog is nervous or over the top try using a T-shirt to help him settle

• Calming band

The calming band (p.100) is a definite must-have for all those vocal dogs that can make the nurses' ears drums bleed! It can also help a dog to feel more relaxed.

Posture, behaviour and tension patterns

Understanding how posture relates to and directly influences behaviour in animals can give you valuable information about how and why your dog reacts the way he does in certain situations. It can also be a helpful tool when working with rescue dogs or selecting a dog from the shelter when details about his background may be sketchy or completely unknown. You can use these observations to learn more about the dog already in your care, a client's dog, or to assess a dog's suitability for the lifestyle that you lead. Even if you are choosing a puppy, understanding the correlation between posture and behaviour can give you some indication as to how he will mature, as many traits and behavioural characteristics are in place at a very early age.

George is already carrying tension through his neck and hindquarters, which contribute to his concern about being contained and handled

What are tension patterns?

Tension patterns are areas of tightness that exist in an animal's body. They may be obvious and inhibit his natural movement to a greater or lesser degree or they may be subtle and less easily detected. Either way they will have an effect on the way the animal functions on an emotional, mental and physical level. In dogs, they can influence not only how the dog thinks, feels and learns but can hamper his ability to be trained and adapt to new situations.

By understanding how tension patterns influence a dog's mind, you can prevent or overcome many common behavioural problems and tailor your management of him to suit his individual needs. Whatever the origin of the tension patterns, with awareness and bodywork and groundwork exercises you can help your canine companion move into a more balanced physical state that will not only enhance your relationship with your dog but improve his overall health and wellbeing as well.

This Jack Russell is tight through the hindquarters and has a rigid tail

…This tension pattern can be linked to dogs that jump up, are always on the go…

…and are wary of contact around their hindquarters

Why do tension patterns occur?

Tension patterns can arise from:

Injury – As well as reducing tolerance levels, pain can alter a dog's normal posture and movement. Lameness and pain are often overlooked in cats and dogs. A high proportion of the animals with defensive behaviours that I have worked with have shown a consistent problem with sensitivity, gait irregularities and/or tension arising from medical issues, immobility in part or parts of the skeleton or uneven development of the soft tissue. Even after the injury has healed, the dog may still move in a posture he adopted to compensate for the original problem. He may have to re-learn how to move in a more effective manner since the muscles may have developed unevenly to maintain this posture.

Dogs are at risk of injury not only from an obvious trauma such as an accident but in their day-to-day life. Rough play, even with a dog of the same height, weight and age can cause neck and back problems that may initially go undetected. Being pulled, dragged, hanged or jerked by the collar can also affect the neck and back and

set up issues with collar handling, grooming and the picking up of limbs. This can trigger reactive behaviours to humans and other dogs. Jumping awkwardly into or out of cars or catching a toy while leaping high into the air can also cause problems that may not be apparent at the time.

Medical problems – Changes in hormones, thyroid imbalances, arthritis, hip displasia, reactions to drugs, poor conformation, bony changes and other medical problems may also result in the development of unwanted behaviours. While appropriate veterinary care is paramount, awareness of how the underlying problem may have affected your dog gives you the opportunity to reduce stress and minimize the knock-on effect the issue may have on your dog's posture and behaviour. A sudden change in behaviour can be indicative of a medical problem; for example, sudden noise sensitivity can be linked to the onset of arthritis. A thorough health check by a veterinary surgeon should be carried out if you note a change in your dog's reactions to stimuli.

Trauma – Shock as a result of an accident or an emotional upheaval such as being in kennels, bereavement or change of circumstance can cause tension throughout the body. As with humans, even low levels of stress can cause physiological changes and influence the dog in his day-to-day existence.

Management and diet – A lack of exercise and/or appropriate activities, over-stimulation, mixed messages from different family members or handlers, an inappropriate environment or unsuitable training methods can all cause stress in a dog and exacerbate habitual and instinctive behaviour.

Bald patches and a poor coat can be linked to stress, over-developed muscles and poor nutrition

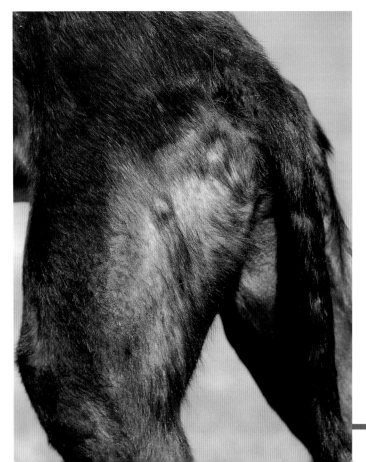

Gentle TTouch work can help calm and settle a dog and teach him that contact can be enjoyable

Poor nutrition and food allergies can affect the body by setting up tension through the neck, back, hindquarters and stomach. Nutritional imbalances or intolerances can also influence behaviour and the ability to learn. In humans, poor nutrition can result in joint pain or muscles that are sore; even the lightest contact may be too much to bear. It stands to reason that the same might apply to our canine companions. Consulting a vet who has specialized in nutrition and who can suggest the appropriate diet and supplements for your dog will have far-reaching benefits and enable him to lead a longer and healthier life.

Here is a short example: Glen, a Border Collie, was extremely wary and reactive to contact on his body by anyone other than his owner. His movement was very short and choppy and his coat was swirly and coarse. I suggested his owner Lorraine speak to Nick Thompson (p.6) and the staff from Higher Nature – a wonderful company that sells superb supplements for dogs – as behaviour like Glen's can often be attributed to lack of nutrients. A week later I received the following email:

> *Dear Sarah*
>
> *I have put Glen on some supplements: MSM, cod-liver oil and glucosamine, and changed his diet to one of fresh cooked food chicken, rice, veg, fish, and so on. What a difference in just a week! His coat has changed and is now smooth, flat and shiny and his temper seems to be better – no mood swings so far.*
>
> *Thanks for your help. I will keep you up-to-date on his progress. Maybe next time we meet you may be able to touch him, deep down he would love to be able to allow that. Lorraine*

And then a while later:

> *Just a quick update on Glen. He is still improving and really surprised me the other day when he went up to a friend for a fuss – totally unheard of before. Lorraine*

Born that way – Some dogs present tension patterns from birth. Puppies with higher levels of tension through their body or in specific parts of their body will generally be more vocal and more demanding, even at a few days old. Unless these tension patterns are reduced, it is likely that the problems will grow as the puppy matures. By working with your puppy using observations and gentle body TTouches you can find any areas that may trigger a reaction in the pup and become aware of his postural habits. You can then take appropriate steps to help your pup mature into a happy, confident and healthy dog.

Conformation can also give you information about how a dog is likely to behave. A dog that is very straight through the neck, back, hindquarters and tail will tend to carry more tension through the body and may therefore be more reactive or unsure than a dog that has more definition through the hind leg and a more relaxed topline. A dog that has a narrow frame can be different in his responses to a dog that has more bone, although this may not always be the case. Dogs with a small, refined frame may have more of a tendency to express their concerns by shying away from something that causes concern, while a dog with a broader head and more bone will tend to become more pushy and boisterous if unsure.

Rough play – even with a dog of the same weight and height – can cause soft tissue damage

ASSESS YOUR DOG

There are three main ways to start the assessment process: look, listen and feel. If you are not accustomed to studying dogs in this way, start with some simple points such as his head carriage and the way he holds his tail. Don't be disheartened if things don't jump out at you straight away. Like developing any new skill, assessment requires practice and some people are naturally more adept at using their eyes than others. It is like learning a new language and the whole picture will emerge as you start piecing the basics together. Make notes on a daily or weekly basis, be open-minded and above all stay positive. Far from looking at the dog in a critical manner, the aim is to get to know and understand your dog on a whole new level. By being aware of the original habits you will know when they have changed.

Look – postural observations

Postural patterns link to a dog's behaviour and character in many ways, and with experience it is possible to gather enough information from the way a dog moves, stands, sits and lies down to form an overall picture of him and greater understanding of how he is likely to respond in a variety of situations.

Try to get into the habit of spending time simply observing your dog. Remember that you are merely making observations and that there is no such thing as a symmetrical dog. All dogs, like all humans, have an uneven posture and a stronger and weaker side.

Keep your eyes soft by using your peripheral vision rather than simply staring at your dog. Watch the dog for a moment and then blink or look away. This often enables you to see more. Film your dog moving if you can and play the film back in slow motion as well as at normal speed.

Although you may notice a lot during the first observations keep checking in with the dog to ensure that it is a true pattern and not

Note whether your dog stands square or with one leg out to the side

This GSD bitch has very weak hindquarters. Note the raised hair over her neck and shoulders

Watch how your dog sits. Molly is sitting on her left hip

just the way he has moved or stood at any particular moment in time.

Make your initial observations in a neutral place such as around the home and in the garden. See if anything changes when he is out and about, when he is going into the vet's surgery or the groomer's salon or when he is exposed to noises, is travelling in a car and so on.

Watch his body language and movement when he is greeting people or dogs that are familiar to him and how they alter when he is exposed to dogs and people that he has not met before. Note whether he changes his behaviour if he is around young or older dogs. Well-socialized, confident dogs will often vary the way they interact with different breeds and with different age groups.

Sitting or lying down

Spend some time watching your dog around the home, his kennel or his run. Note how he sits and how he lies down. Does he always sit on the same hip? Does he sit with his hind limbs forward or out to the side? Can he sit? Does he always lie on the same side? When he gets up, does the movement look graceful and effortless or does he struggle to get to his feet?

The tail

Look at his tail. Does it wag quickly or slowly? Does it wag consistently or only at certain times? Can he move his tail from the base to the tip or is part of the tail rigid and fixed? Look at the set of the tail. Does it hang down, or is it held tightly up in the air? Is the tail carried straight out like a banner or is it tucked firmly between the hind legs? Does the tail wag more to the left or the right or does it move evenly in both directions? When your dog is moving does the set of his tail change? Does the tail now move in a circular manner like a rotor blade or does it move more to one side than the other?

Look at the set of the tail. A curly tail will usually curl towards the lower hip

Note whether the way he sits is a habitual pattern or if the dog changes from time to time. Barney alternates between his right and left hip, which is common with dogs that have a docked tail

On the move

When the dog is moving, look for a free and even gait in walk and trot. Does he walk calmly and in balance or does he rush around and do everything at speed? Is he reluctant to move even when asked? Does he pace?

When your dog is running does he bunny hop with his hind legs or is he free and moving equally through both hips and hind limbs? Does he curve his body more to one side than the other (crabbing) or run with his head tilted to the left or to the right? If the dog is moving in a curve, say for example, to the right, does his head and body move in the direction of the arc or does he actually carry his head and neck to the left?

On the lead

Note his responses when his lead is put on. Does he leap about in excitement or stand patiently with a gentle slow wag of the tail? Does he go into freeze (p.18) or does he lower his body to the ground licking his lips with his tail tucked between his legs? When walking outside on the leash, note whether he is happy and moves in a relaxed and easy manner. Or does he seem concerned and rush along without stopping to sniff or urinate and with his ears flat or folded back against his head? Does he drag you along with his ears up and with hard staring eyes, watching for dogs/people/cats/cars?

Can he walk in a straight line or does he cower and 'hug' the ground? Does he spin, leap or pull, and tuck himself in behind you or does he stop and start? Can he actually walk on the leash or does he go into freeze or lie down? Is he stiff? Is there a curve through his body or does the footfall of his hind limbs follow the direction of his front paws?

Switch sides so that the dog is now on your other side and run through the observations again. Some dogs are totally thrown by this seemingly simple task, particularly if they have been trained and handled, as is traditional, from a person's left side.

If possible, enlist the help of a friend or colleague to lead the dog away from you and towards you. Note whether your dog is happy to

Molly is stiff through her hips and hind legs. She swings her barrel more to the left when she walks and her tail is carried like a banner to help her balance

Look at your dog on the move. Look to see whether there is equal movement through the hindlegs or whether one looks stiffer than the other. How is the tail carried? Is it more to the right or more to the left? Does it change?

Even when Molly stands her tail is still rigid, which links to the tension in her back and hindquarters

When the dog is running free, note how he turns. Archie is turning his head in the direction that he is moving

be led away from you by another person. When walking towards you does he pull and rush so that he can get to you more quickly?

Look at his head, ear and tail carriage. Are they straight, upright, low or unlevel? Look at his ribcage and belly. Are they evenly developed on both sides or does he carry them more to the left or to the right?

If you are working with your dog on a path or concreted area watch for any paw prints that your dog may be leaving. Sweaty pads may be a sign of stress, but can also be simply the sign of a hot dog, so don't jump to conclusions straight away. Take the ambient temperature into account and watch to see if he cools down once he is out and about.

Molly carries her head slightly to the left even though she is moving to the right

Does he hang away from the handler?

Egan is standing with his hind limbs underneath him. He looks weak through the hips and lower back

Standing still

If he will do so, ask your dog to stand while you look at his posture and the way he is muscled through the body. Does he have a good, well-defined topline or does he look weak and poorly developed? Does he stand with his neck and tail high and his back slightly dropped or with his head and tail low? Is the muscle development even through his neck, forequarters, back and hindquarters or is he more developed on one side of his body?

When you look down on his back does it look as though the ribs are level or does one side of the ribcage appear more open or further back than the other?

Observe the way in which he holds himself and organizes his limbs when standing. Does he stand square with his weight evenly distributed through each limb or does he stand with one or more limbs out to the side or forward or back? Does he stand base narrow or base wide (with his feet closely together or wide apart)? Does he

Look at the muscling on the dog's hindquarters – most dogs are more developed on one side than the other

This greyhound is under-muscled. His topline is weak

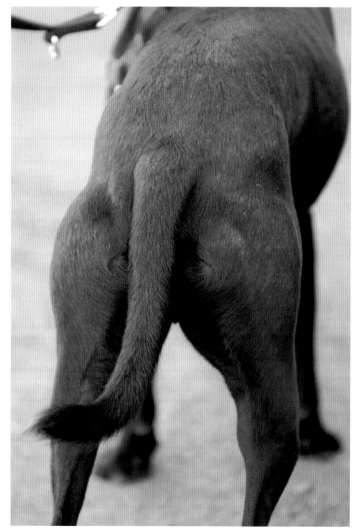

Can he stand square or does he stand with one leg outstretched?

stand with his limbs forwards or back? Note whether this changes depending on your own position. Some dogs will lean more towards the side that their owner/handler is standing on.

Can he stand quietly or does he continuously shift his weight from side to side or become agitated when asked to be still?

If it is not threatening for the dog, look at him head-on and study the height, shape and set of his facial features. Look for worry or stress lines across the muzzle. Holly has worry lines along her muzzle and across the top of her head. Her ears are very tense

Look at the position of his head on his neck. Is it straight or does it have a slight tilt?

Face-on

If you know the dog well and you know he will not feel threatened or be tempted to jump up, stand in front of him and look at him head-on. Is his head straight or does he stand with his neck to one side? Do his ears and eyes look level or does one eye and/or ear look higher, further back or bigger than the other? Look at the head. Is the curve of the skull even on both sides or is one side flatter, shorter or higher than the other? Look at his muzzle. Is it level or higher on one side than the other?

Poppy is standing with her weight more on her right legs. Note whether your dog habitually stands with his weight more on one side than the other or if his balance changes depending on the position of the handler

Toes and skin

Look at the spread of the toes to determine how your dog is distributing his weight through his limbs. If your dog has splayed toes on the outside of his feet, his weight is falling through the outside of his limbs. Check to see whether the toes are straight or if any are crooked. Note whether the toes are even in their appearance or whether one or more look straighter or more arched than the others. Look at his nails to see which ones are shorter or more scuffed. This will also tell you whether he is balanced in his movement or not. You may find that a nail or nails on one foot are more scuffed than the others. If your dog is happy for you to pick up his feet, look at his pads. If the weight distribution is uneven through the body, the pads that are bearing more weight may appear flatter and rounder in shape or may be shinier in appearance than the others.

This dog bears more weight on the outside of his limb. Note how the outer toe is splayed away from the others

Look at the spread of his toes to determine how he distributes his weight through his limbs

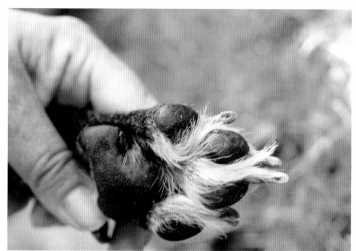

Uneven weight distribution can also be seen on the pads. The outer pads have a shiny patch showing there is more wear on this part of the foot

Look at the colour of the dog's gums, the whites of the eyes, and the skin on his stomach, inner thigh and between his toes. Dogs that are stressed or that have an internal imbalance including food allergies will often have red gums, eyes and skin. They may have glazed, staring eyes, bark excessively, may be restless and/or extremely volatile.

Molly is an anxious dog and barks excessively. She has red gums and a red tongue, which can be indicative of an aroused or agitated dog

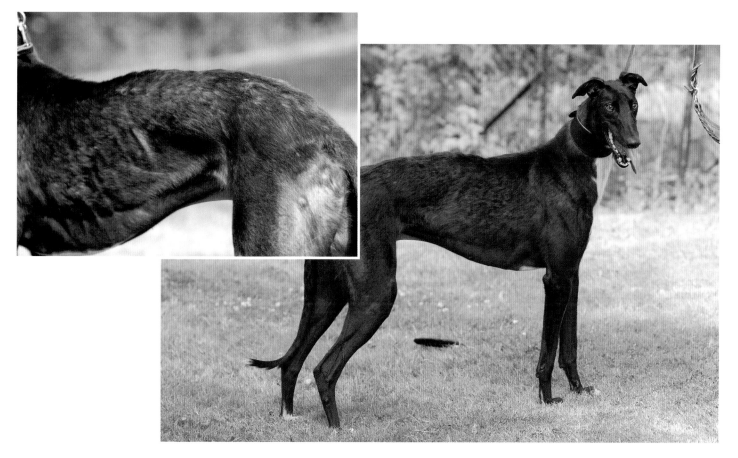

This greyhound has a very poor coat. He is bald in some areas and his coat is dry and scurfy. Note the dry raised areas on this dog's back (right). This is linked to tension and reduced mobility through the lower back and hindquarters

The coat

You can also glean a lot of information about a dog's general health and mobility by studying his coat. A coat that is dry all over or in large patches is an indication that the dog is deficient in nutrients, is stressed, has tension through the neck and/or back or is unwell.

Look for hair that stands up, seems greasy, rough or dry, particularly around the neck, hindquarters and back. Check to see if there are any areas where dandruff or scurf is present, which may be indicative of tight skin or tension through that part of the body.

Make a note of the swirls in the coat, particularly if they seem excessive in places. Although they may be part of the dog's natural coat, they may also change as he releases tension through the body. They can also indicate the onset of a potential problem or appear after surgery or an accident.

Look at the direction in which the coat lies, particularly over the shoulders, lower back and over the hips. Where the hips are unlevel, the hair on the hindquarters will tend to lie in the direction of the lower hip; and the hair at the base of the neck and over the withers will tend to fall towards whichever shoulder is lower. If the hair seems

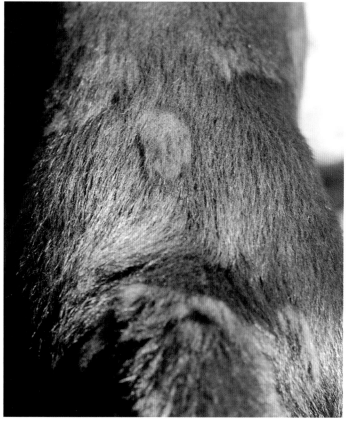

to run the wrong way, which is against the natural lie of the coat it may be indicative of an old trauma such as a fracture.

Note the general colour and vitality of the coat. A dog with a black coat or black patches may develop brown shading in the black, which can be linked to underlying tension. If the coat is naturally light, look for areas that may have darkened or appear discoloured. After bodywork and/or dietary alterations the patches often change back to the normal colour of the coat, unless of course they are part of the dog's natural shading or markings.

Look for white marks or white lines that are unrelated to the natural colouring of the dog. They can be the sign of an old injury and may explain why your dog is concerned by certain situations or why he is unable to maintain a sit stay or dislikes travelling in the car.

Also note if your dog has less coat on one side than the other. Bald patches or areas where the skin has less hair cover can be indicative of how your dog habitually sits or sleeps, or points to excessive tension carried on one side.

When the dog is shedding, look for any unusual patterns that may highlight an area where there is reduced mobility through the soft tissue. A dog may hold onto the coat in areas where there is more tension through the skin. Excessive or persistent shedding can be a sign of stress, and you may note that although your dog appears calm on the outside when people come to the house, he drops his coat

while the visitors are present. If your dog continues to drop his coat over a period of time take him to your vet as this may be caused by a medical problem. Even if your dog does not have any behavioural or health concerns, it can be beneficial to observe his natural coat pattern so that you know if anything changes for him. If there is an underlying health concern, the coat will usually be one of the first things to alter.

Tyler has a line of white hairs over each hip indicative of an old injury or tension through the pelvis. As his posture slowly improves the white hairs are diminishing

Chili was born with deformed feet. He developed a feather swirl behind his right shoulder after surgery. The coat is also slightly lighter in this area

Look for any unusual patterns when the dog sheds his coat. Sally has patches of dry old coat over her hindquarters

Look for areas where there is less hair cover – note the worn area on this dog's thigh. This can be indicative of over-developed muscles or can be linked to the habitual sitting or lying patterns of the dog

Other observations

Many dogs that have the coat changes mentioned are reactive when these areas are touched. As a result, they may be labelled as unpredictable because they may bite in some instances when being handled and not in others. In these circumstances, the unreliability comes not from the dog but the inconsistent way in which he may inadvertently be being handled and touched. By being aware of

Although Molly is a chocolate Labrador her coat is lighter in several areas, including her tail, which can be linked to tension in the skin

any coat change you can assess how you might be able to start working successfully with your dog, without triggering any unwanted behaviours by mistake.

Watch how your dog responds to every situation and learn how he uses his body language to express himself. Note how he eats. Dogs that are over the top and carry tension around the muzzle tend to snatch at food and treats, while dogs that are timid may eat more delicately and be more easily distracted when feeding. A dog that is tight or weak through the lower back and hips may find it hard to squat when going to the loo. He may have to creep forward as he urinates or may be unable to cock a specific leg.

Listen

Pay attention to any noise your dog makes, such as excessive sighing, panting or whining, which can indicate stress. Listen to whether he blows through his lips when concerned, or if he coughs or hiccups when pressure is applied to his collar. Note whether he whines when trying to get up or even when he is lying in his bed. Listening to the footfall of the dog can tell you how he is distributing his weight through his limbs. He may land more heavily on a particular limb or may scuff the floor with one or more of his feet.

Meg

Meg is a Border Collie who was adopted from a working farm when she was three months old. Although she was slightly wary of strangers, she enjoyed human contact and was particularly bonded to the neighbour's son. At 16 months old her behaviour changed dramatically – almost overnight – and her owner, Sue, contacted me in a bid to help her dog. Instead of rushing up to the boy when she saw him, Meg had started growling and appeared to be stalking the child. This behaviour coincided with an excessive and sudden fear of loud noises.

These behaviours could have been explained as typical of a Collie, but although the natural instincts of any dog should be taken into account, it is all too easy to jump to conclusions and focus purely on training to overcome the problems, rather than look for the underlying cause. Sue had been on one of my workshops when she first adopted Meg, so knew

that there might be something else that had triggered such a dramatic and worrying alteration in her dog. I asked Sue if she had seen any change in Meg's coat and she said that the hair over her back and quarters had become extremely curly and coarse. I recommended Meg be seen by a vet and a week later I received a call from a relieved Sue. Meg had been examined and x-rayed by her vet who found new bone developing in her hocks.

Fortunately Meg's vet was happy to refer her to a holistic vet who suggested some dietary supplements, and gave her a course of acupressure (see p.91) backed up with homeopathic remedies. Sue also used TTouch to maintain the changes that were being made with the acupressure and Meg quickly returned to her former self. Within two weeks of starting treatment she was back playing happily with the little boy and her noise sensitivity had diminished.

Feel

If you know the dog or if the dog you are working with is happy to be handled by unfamiliar people, you can use your hands to confirm or give you a more specific feel as to where the tension lies. Feel for temperature changes, coarse or rough hair, tight skin or areas that trigger the muscles to spasm or twitch. Check to see if the dog has any lumps or bumps and note whether the muscles are developed equally on both sides. Feel for any areas where the soft tissue seems weak or tight and areas where the skin may dip or feel hollow under your fingers.

Flat-hand assessment

Checking the dog like this is called a flat-hand assessment. When carrying out the exploration, your hands become your eyes. The assessment should be slow and considered. The aim is to read the dog through your fingers. If you rush, you may miss subtle

Run your hands lightly and slowly over the dog's body. Watch his reactions at all times

If it is safe to do so, use your hands to glean more information about the dog. This little white dog is tight through the back. Hand contact in this area is triggering him to arch his back and raise a hind leg

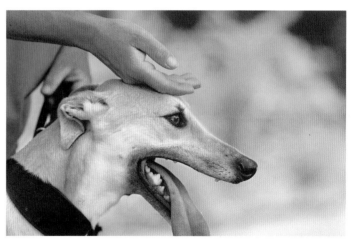

Use the back of your hand if the dog is shy or worried by hand contact

If he is threatened by contact on his head, start on his shoulder. Despite temperatures of nearly 40℃ (104°F), this dog begins to soften and lick his lips instead of panting

Feel for temperature changes in areas that are tight…

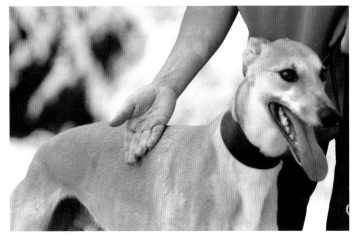

…or where the coat feels coarse

Check the temperature of the lower legs and feet. Nervous dogs often dislike contact on their legs and may have cold or cooler paws

When this dog's hindleg is lifted he braces and hunches through the back in compensation

responses and slight temperature changes and only pick up every 'third word', which means that areas that are giving the dog cause for concern when touched may go undetected.

If the dog is happy to be touched, start at the head and run the flat of your hand smoothly and lightly along his neck and back. Continue along the shoulder and side, and down the front and hind limbs. Once you have finished one side, check the other and note if your findings are the same on both sides. Stop immediately if the dog is worried or unsure. If he is shy or nervous, especially around his neck, start on the side of the shoulder and try using the back of your hand instead. This is less threatening for the dog and it may also help you to be more aware of changes in temperature.

Lift each leg slowly in turn. If he is weighting one limb more than the others it may be impossible for him to raise a leg when asked to or he may keep that limb rigid indicating tension in the shoulder or hindquarters.

Watch the dog for his reactions at all times. He may express concern by moving away, sitting down, rolling over onto his back, licking his lips, yawning, fooling around or freezing (p.18) or growling.

What to do next

If you find tension or areas that are weak or where the animal lacks awareness of his body there is plenty that you can do to alleviate the problem. However, if you suspect an underlying physical problem, it is vital to consult a veterinary surgeon and to follow his or her advice about suitable adjustments to the environment and management of the dog before using the methods in this book.

The methods described here make it possible to produce a very rapid difference in a dog's behaviour and attitude to life. However, depending on the longevity of the problem and/or the underlying cause, it is important to be realistic and bear in mind that some tension patterns may take time and patience to fully address.

Work through the next few pages to find out more about the types of problems tension and discomfort can bring to specific parts of

the body and then go on to use the variety of ground exercises and TTouches in 'Taking steps to help your dog (pp.74–121) to help to improve body awareness, function and posture in your dog. These are designed to offer the dog a new experience. Although we are often taught from an early age that we must work hard in order to achieve results, this is not necessarily true or appropriate when working with TTouch. It is easy to get carried away and throw every available piece of equipment on the dog as well as launching into a full bodywork session but this can totally overload him by flooding his nervous system with too much information. It is important to remember that the nervous system responds to the lightest of touches and the smallest of movements. Developing a quiet and observant approach in ourselves can be instrumental in producing a more balanced temperament in a dog, which in turn can help to eliminate many undesirable behaviour patterns.

It doesn't take hours of work to elicit a change. Sometimes a few gentle lifts and slides (see pp.95–97) and one or two slow walking exercises (for example, Weaving through cones, p.105, or Uneven poles, p.110) can be enough to make a significant change in the first session. If we are asking the dog to quieten his behaviour then surely we should be doing the same? Several short sessions through the day or over the course of a few days are far more beneficial than one long session, whatever your methods of training. By adopting this approach you allow the dog time to take on board everything that you are asking him to do and he can process the information during the breaks. It is often during the time out or sometimes the day after the TTouch session that you see a shift in a dog's posture and behaviour.

Holly is highly stressed and pulls

Some simple ear work (see p.103) enables Holly to settle and focus, and her whole expression softens

Walking Holly using two-point contact begins to calm her down

Working around the mouth can be very calming and…

…relaxing

The muzzle

The mouth is linked to learning. When humans concentrate, they often chew pens or fingertips or may lick or bite their lips. Babies of any mammal species often place items in their mouths. The mouth is also linked to the limbic system. This is the area of the brain that is considered to be the control centre for the emotions and the gateway to learning (described by Daniel Goleman, in his book *Emotional Intelligence*). This emotional connection is consistent with the early observations made by Linda Tellington Jones (p.8) that many animals improve in their behaviour and in their ability to operate in a calm and focused mode once tension in the mouth is reduced. Working around the mouth, both inside and out stimulates the salivary glands, and triggers the relaxation-promoting parasympathetic nervous system (see p.14), which in turn quietens the sympathetic nervous system, responsible for the fight, flight or freeze responses (pp.18–19).

The mouth is one of the most important parts of the dog's body as dogs use their mouths to communicate with a variety of signals including curling their lips, licking their lips, blowing, panting, yawning, growling, vocalizing and mouthing.

Mouth work can help to reduce excessive mouthing and chewing…

Indicators of tension in the mouth

Dogs with tension around the muzzle may also:

- Fixate on food/toys
- Be clingy
- Find it hard to relax
- Crave constant attention
- Dislike contact around the head and muzzle
- Find it hard to accept a headcollar
- Vocalize
- Have a short concentration span
- Be reactive to other dogs

…and is extremely beneficial for teething puppies

Dogs with tension around the muzzle will often bark, pant and mouth. They may also obsess about food

Dogs with tension around the muzzle are often easily distracted

Dogs that have narrow muzzles such as sight-hounds may have more of a tendency towards sensitivity and shyness than their broader-nosed counterparts. Over-exaggerated mouth movements tend to be more typical in the broader-muzzled breeds such as the Retrievers or Bull breeds, although this information should be taken as a guide rather than as a definite rule of thumb.

The effects of muzzle tension

Dogs can carry a lot of tension around the muzzle and jaw, just like people. If a dog carries tension in and around the mouth, his ability to communicate may be limited. Some dogs with tension around the mouth may be overly sensitive and emotional. They may have a tendency to go off their food when upset and may be reluctant to take food from people if unsure of the situation. They may lick their lips rapidly to express concern and their eyes may be glassy with a vacant expression. If cornered or pushed too far they may have a tendency to nip out of nervousness without a warning growl although they will have offered many signals first to express their concern (see p.17).

Dogs with tension around the muzzle may also bark, drink, pant and mouth excessively and may show a particular interest or obsession with food, toys and other articles. They may be quick to

arouse and prone to hyperactive behaviour. They can be slow to mature mentally and emotionally. They may be boisterous, pushy and over the top and may alternate between being totally full on and fast asleep. If forced beyond their comfort zone or if 'fool around' behaviour is stopped through force, they may mouth hard and/or grab the handler's clothing or the lead. In the extreme, they may bite.

If they can take food from a person, such dogs may snatch the treats from the hand as tension through the jaw limits their ability to be subtle in their movement. Lines or wrinkles across the nose will often accompany tension around the muzzle. Hormonal imbalance can also give rise to tension around the mouth.

Observing the way a dog holds his muzzle and jaw can give you vital information about how he is coping with a situation. A still, tense mouth and jaw can be a signal that the dog has 'shut down' and gone into freeze. Blowing through the lips or frequent lip licking can also indicate concern. The saliva can be an indicator of how a dog feels. Excessive saliva can be linked to gut function and extreme stress while a dry mouth may be an indicator of a nervous dog.

Ollie lacks focus and finds it hard to walk on a lead when in a new situation. He goes into 'fool around' and grabs the leash when he is unsure

Excessive saliva can also be a sign of stress or poor gut function

Direct eye contact can be very threatening for a dog. Holly is highly agitated

The eyes are the window to the soul. Everything about the beautiful Poppy tells you she is happy, friendly and contented

The eyes, ears and head

Eyes

The eyes really are the windows to the soul. Dogs that are easy to handle and even-tempered generally have soft, appealing eyes with richness and depth to the colour, while tension and stress will result in a hard, glassy eye that appears bulging, glazed or unblinking. The skin around the eye may be tight and wrinkled with stress lines under the eye giving the dog a pinched look and furrowed brow.

Dogs use their eyes to communicate. They may blink or move their eye sideways or down to give information to other dogs or people. Rolling an eye can be a sign of concern. Looking at any dog directly in the eye can be unsettling for the dog and can trigger unwanted responses. If nervous and prone to flight (p.18), the dog will look away and avoid direct eye contact. If he is unable to remove himself from the situation he may nip out of fear or start shaking. Direct eye contact can also trigger a dog to jump up or lunge forward. Breaking eye contact by looking away or keeping your eyes soft when observing or interacting with dogs will reduce their stress levels and allow them to process what you are teaching them.

Hard eyes are often accompanied by tension across the forehead and around the temporomandibular joint (TMJ). Dogs that are nervous may have raised eyebrows and wide or staring eyes. This can also be linked to anxiety and a genuine fear of being left alone.

Ears

The ears are also very important in dog communication. The set of the ear will give you information about how your dog feels and can be an early warning sign of mounting stress. Dogs that are noise-sensitive, reactive to other dogs and people and/or suffer from travel sickness often carry tension through the ears.

Cold ear tips can be an indicator of stress/anxiety levels and may be accompanied by cold feet. They can be linked to tension in the neck and a higher than average respiration and heart rate. Dogs that are in shock or dogs that have suffered some trauma will often have cold ear tips. Shock can kill, and TTouch ear work (p.103) has saved the lives of many animals that have been injured or who are sick by preventing them from going into shock while veterinary attention was being sought. There are many acupressure points throughout the ear relating to the rest of the body (see p.91 for information on

Dogs that are tight around the base of the ears are often in a constant state of alertness and find it hard to relax

THE EYES, EARS AND HEAD

acupressure). If there is pain or injury elsewhere in the body there may be a sensitive spot somewhere on the ear.

High-set ears can be associated with very reactive behaviour. In certain breeds such as Collies, Lurchers and German Shepherds the ears may touch on the top of the head. Dogs with this tension pattern are often very excitable with little or no attention span. They can be difficult to train as movement easily distracts them. Ears that are flat and/or folded can indicate shyness and nervousness. As with a high ear set, flat or folded ears can be linked to noise sensitivity and are often accompanied by tension around the hindquarters and tail. Crooked ears or ears that appear to be set unevenly on the head can point to tension through the neck and/or jaw. The dog may be very reactive to contact here and may dislike having his collar handled.

Many people naturally stroke their dog's ears but some dogs may have developed a phobia about this sort of contact due to medical problems that required a long period of medication. Constant

scratching can also cause thickening of the ear and may make a dog protective about being handled around the head.

Tension in the ears will affect any tension across the top of the head and vice versa. Some dogs are so tense that their ears feel as though there are bands of rigid plastic around the base. They may be very reactive and may dislike contact on, or movement near the head. Dogs with tight ears may also have a hot spot on the top of the head, over the withers and approximately two-thirds of the way along the back. Red gums, red eyes and red skin around the foot pads and on the belly may accompany these tension patterns.

Teaching any dog to accept and enjoy contact around the ears is extremely beneficial not just in terms of gaining tools to help him to settle and relax but in order that you can carry out regular health checks without causing any distress. If you do have to treat his ears at any time, you can use the ear work before and after administering the drops to help him stay calm during the necessary treatment.

Crooked or uneven ears can be linked to tension through the jaw and neck

From behind it is clear that the ears and neck are uneven in this greyhound

Head

Dogs with a small head and/or a high dome can be slow to learn. They tend to be more reactive in their responses to new or threatening situations. With awareness and quiet, consistent handling and training, dogs with a small head can move beyond their instinctive responses through increased levels of self-confidence and self-control.

There is a correlation between the forehead and the stomach, and dogs that are tight across the brow can suffer digestive disturbances or go off their food when unsettled. Food intolerances or poor gut function can in turn give rise to anxious behaviour and dogs with tension across the head will often be whiney and clingy.

Some dogs have a hot spot in the middle of the head. This is often accompanied by reddening of the membranes in the mouth and around the eyes, and the dog may have a tendency to lunge and bite when feeling threatened. It is usually a sign of stress and the dog may be constantly on the go. He may fluctuate between extremes – being either compulsive and over the top or asleep.

Indicators of tension in the eyes, ears and head

Dogs with tension around the eyes, ears and head may also:

- Have a stiff or uneven gait
- Find it hard to adapt to new situations
- Find it hard to lower or raise their head
- Be nervous about travelling in a car
- Be wary of strangers and new dogs
- Rush or freeze when asked to move
- Be in a constant state of alert
- Be noise-sensitive
- Be protective over toys and/or food
- Be overly intense and crave attention
- Have a short concentration span
- Find it hard to relax
- Have an elevated heart rate
- Dislike being touched

Dogs with tension around the head, eyes and ears…　　*…will often pull when on the lead*

This greyhound has tension in the neck…

…which is linked to tension in the fore and hindquarters

The neck

The neck is made up of seven cervical vertebrae. Tension in the neck influences and is influenced by tension in the shoulders, back and hindquarters.

Dogs that bite are often extremely uncomfortable in the neck and may need physiotherapy, cranio-sacral therapy or gentle osteopathic work to help them overcome their problems. This discomfort can be set up at an early age if a puppy is dragged by his collar or at any point if the dog is pulled or checked roughly on the leash. Excessive rough or over-energetic play or falling over when running loose can cause problems in both the neck and back. Damage to the soft tissue or skeleton may not be obvious at first but if your dog undergoes even a slight change in his character take him to a vet for a thorough examination.

Any issues such as growling, fooling around, grabbing the lead or freezing when the collar or lead is put on or taken off may also be linked to problems in the neck. In these cases, the dog's shoulders and back should also be checked. Such responses aren't always the result of soft tissue or skeletal damage, but may be a sign of stress and tension, which can be dramatically reduced with gentle bodywork and groundwork.

Tension in the neck can affect visual and vestibular balance and the dog may be highly aroused or extremely sensitive to movement and noise. He may be concerned by shape changes and be wary of walking through doorways or narrow spaces since tension in the neck may affect spatial awareness. If the first two cervical vertebrae (C1 and C2) are affected, the dog may appear as though his ears are uneven and it may look as though the top of his head is narrower on one side than the other. He may have a head tilt and may be sensitive to contact through the TMJ (see p.58). As with humans, tension in

Dogs that bite or panic when on the lead are often uncomfortable in the neck

Tension in the neck can make a dog react to contact in this part of his body

Touching Ollie on the neck triggers more 'fool around' behaviour

the neck can impair learning and the dog may find it difficult to concentrate and/or retain information.

Dogs with uneven muscling through the neck may find it harder to turn in one direction than the other. When asked to walk in a curve such a dog may lead with his shoulder and tilt his head in the opposite direction. If the dog reacts to being led, note which side triggers more reactive behaviours. Some dogs are naturally concerned about being handled from their left side as this is often non-habitual for dogs and people, but tension in the neck may be the cause as it may be uncomfortable for the dog to look in the direction of their handler. The dog may then associate the discomfort with the presence of a person on that side and continue to have concerns about being led on a specific side long after the discomfort has gone.

Tension in the neck affects movement through the entire body including the front limbs. It also affects balance and proprioception (see p.14), and dogs with this tension pattern may be clumsy or pull excessively on the leash. They may knock agility jumps with a front limb or limbs and, as there is a close correlation between the neck and the hindquarters, may also have a lower hip or scuff the ground with one hind foot.

Indicators of tension in the neck

Dogs with tension in the neck may also:
- React to being touched on the top of the head
- Be concerned about having their jaw opened
- React to being injected or microchipped
- Dislike being picked up
- Be concerned about the vet
- Have raised hair on the neck or around the base of the neck
- Bark excessively or not bark at all
- Have skin problems and/or food intolerances

The forequarters

Tension around the shoulders and withers can indicate a dog that lacks confidence and either bullies or retreats as a coping strategy. He may appear distant and aloof and in the extreme may cower or freeze before biting if a sudden move is made towards his collar. The hair around the base of his neck and over the shoulders may be raised and may feel rough and coarse.

Dogs that are tight behind the shoulder blades often have a high chase drive and may find it hard to focus as they are permanently on the lookout or are distracted by movement. They may leap and spin when on the lead and may find walking to heel an impossible task. Tension in the shoulders is also common in dogs that pull. This may be accompanied by tension at the top of the tail.

Tension through the chest and shoulders will affect movement through the front limbs. The dog may have a short stride or an uneven gait. He may find it difficult to move in a particular direction and may have uneven muscling in these areas. The breastbone may lean more to the left or the right and the dog may be fixed through the withers and back. Tension through the front limbs and wrists can also be linked to tension in the neck.

Indicators of tension in the forequarters

Dogs with tension through the forequarters may also:

- React to having their front limbs touched or lifted
- Find it hard to jump
- Be nervous about walking over slippery surfaces
- Freeze or become hyperactive when wearing a harness
- Have cold feet and pads
- Scuff the ground with their front feet
- Paw at their owner or other dogs
- Be sensitive to contact on the ribs
- Dislike being contained

This German Shepherd is over-developed through the neck and shoulders and is weak through the hindquarters. As a result she lacks confidence…

She also finds it hard to be on a lead and move in balance. She alternates between leaping in the air…

…and shies away from the handler

…and lying down

This dog is very tight through the back and lacks movement through the shoulders and hips

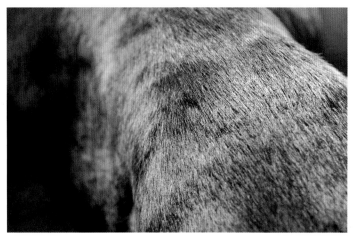

He has unlevel hips and a small area of raised hair in front of each hip joint

The back

The back is made up of 13 thoracic vertebrae. A well-defined topline, a flexible spine and good core strength are important for the overall health and wellbeing of the dog. When studying a dog's back you may notice a slight dip just behind the back of the shoulder blades. This can be a vulnerable area for dogs particularly when they are young, old or have under-developed back muscles.

When the neck and head is raised, the back drops. Pressure on the neck can therefore weaken or cause discomfort in the back, and dogs with a habitually high head-carriage may be consistently in the flight/ fight reflex becoming excitable or reactive when unsure. Tension in the back can give also give rise to an excessively low head-carriage. Any tension in the back is usually accompanied by tension through the hindquarters, shoulders and neck.

A tight back may also limit the dog's ability to relax, release tension or communicate with people or another dog. Play bowing, rolling around on his back, moving slowly in a curve, stretching, shaking off and so on are important parts of a dog's day-to-day life. If the dog has reduced mobility through the spine he may be unable or feel unable

Being able to shake off…

to express himself in these ways, which can add to any existing levels of concern.

A tight back may lead to the gait being short and choppy and the dog appearing to be stiff or weak through every joint in his body. A high, rigid or excessively clamped tail often accompanies this posture. Dogs with this tension pattern may find it hard to relax and are likely to be in a constant state of alertness, often leaping to their feet at the slightest sound or movement.

When a dog is aroused, the skin on the back naturally tightens and the hackles may rise over the shoulders and lower back. Some dogs carry so much tension through their body that they are habitually in this physical state of arousal. The back muscles may be so tight that they spasm on contact. This tension impairs the circulation in the skin so the coat in this area may look dull, lifeless and scurfy. The hair may also be excessively curly, wavy or raised, although, of course, normal coat patterns should be taken into account.

Dogs with tension through the back may be highly reactive to contact anywhere on their body and may dislike having their collar handled. They may be extremely defensive around strangers and boisterous dogs. They may also be difficult to handle and train as they may find any containment extremely threatening. They may, therefore, overreact to wearing a collar, harnesses or other training equipment and may bite if the handler physically attempts to restrain them.

Do not be fooled by a dog that seems to be extremely flexible and bends his entire body left and right rather than simply wagging his tail when excited. He may still have areas of tension through the shoulders or lower back, which may only be detected by running your hand or back of your hand slowly over the back. This type of dog is often very exuberant and may be slow to mature. He may find it hard to concentrate for long periods of time and will be inclined to play the fool when under pressure.

Tension through the mid-back and lumbar region can trigger sexual behaviour when the dog is patted or stroked in this area. This area can be linked to noise sensitivity and also digestive problems, and the dog may either bolt his food or be reluctant to eat.

…and roll on the back is important for dogs. Both help them to release stress

Indicators of tension in the back

Dogs with tension through the back may also:
- Find it hard to get into or out of the car
- Dislike being towel-dried
- Dislike being groomed
- Be reactive to being picked up
- Be concerned about the vet
- Be defensive when asked to move or leave a comfortable bed
- Be nervous about children
- Find it hard to maintain a good body weight
- Be overly protective
- Pull on the lead or be reluctant to walk
- Bark excessively
- Pace
- Crab (walk with their body in a curve away from the direction of the movement)

A short and choppy gait is often accompanied by a high or tight tail

Tension in the lumbar area can trigger aroused behaviour when the dog is patted or stroked in this area

Samuel Whiskers

Samuel Whiskers is a five-year-old male, mixed breed dog, owned by Sarah Whiffen who works at Battersea Old Windsor. Sam arrived at Battersea when he was two and a half years old. He had been found as a stray. When Sarah first saw Sam he had puncture wounds around his neck from a bite from a large dog. He was extremely nervous and was highly stressed in the kennel, and spent much of his time spinning and leaping in the air. Sam was lucky and was only in the sales block for a few days before being adopted by Sarah.

Sam Whiskers is intelligent, loving and great fun but also extremely nervous, fearful of strangers and hyperactive. He is clingy and constantly seeks physical reassurance. He also has many sound phobias and dislikes being left alone. He used to lunge and bark at strangers, including new visitors to his home, and was unpredictable with other dogs. To enable Sam to develop confidence Sarah takes him to training classes every week. This has been a significant step in helping him to overcome his fear of new people and dogs.

When Sam first came into the garden he was pulling Sarah around the lawn

Assessing Sam

Sarah had attended some of my TTouch workshops at Battersea and had already started to make some observations of Sam at home. She is wonderful with dogs and has a natural talent for working with distressed animals. Sam had already come such a long way but still had obvious levels of concern and Sarah asked if I would give her some help with Sam on a one-to-one basis. As Battersea Old Windsor had kindly allowed us to take photographs of their dogs for this book I suggested that Sam might like to attend the photo shoot.

When Sam came into the garden where we were working, he pulled Sarah around the lawn and barked furiously at Bob, our fantastic photographer. Sam was anxious to stay close to

Sam had a patch of coarse raised hair around the base of his tail, which is common in reactive dogs

Contact on a specific part of Sam's back triggered him…

…to leap to his feet barking furiously

Sarah's partner, and was so agitated he couldn't even stop to sniff or urinate. His body was rigid and his eyes were hard and intense – all signs that he was extremely concerned.

When Sarah began making her careful and slow flat-hand assessment of Sam we noted that he was wary of contact around his beard and muzzle and would politely push Sarah's hand away with a paw if she attempted to touch his face. Sarah confirmed that Sam had never liked to be handled around the muzzle, which is consistent with dogs that are very vocal and have a sensitive temperament.

Sarah also found a hot patch in the middle of Sam's back. The coat around this area was standing up away from his body and felt rougher to the touch; there was also a patch of coarse hair around the base of his tail.

It is vital that the flat-hand assessment is unhurried and that the handler really pays attention to the dog's reactions to pinpoint which areas are giving him cause for concern. As Sarah ran her hand lightly and slowly over Sam's body, she could see that it was contact on a very specific part of his back that triggered him to leap, barking furiously, to his feet. To encourage Sam to settle when he was standing, barking on all fours, I asked Sarah to do gentle back lifts (see p.112) to release and soften his topline. Quietly changing a dog's posture is far more effective than simply trying to stop the

Gentle back lifts helped to release and soften Sam's topline, which helped him to quieten and settle

behaviour, provided it is safe to touch him when he is agitated.

I was pleased with what Sarah had been able to see and feel in her assessment, as everything she described fitted his behaviour profile. Not only did the observations give Sarah a clear idea of how she could begin to work with Sam, but they would also serve as a barometer of how he might be progressing. If his coat and posture began to alter, his behaviour should follow suit.

Helping Sam

Over the two sessions Sam underwent remarkable changes. He became visibly more relaxed as Sarah worked over his back, and the tension in his hindquarters began to diminish. By using Clouded Leopard TTouches (p.96) around his head, Sarah could work around Sam's muzzle and on his beard, which helped to prepare him for wearing a calming band (see p.100).

Once Sam was happy with the calming band he progressed to a head collar (see p.84). Taking a dog calmly through the steps to wearing a head collar can be a vital part of the rehabilitation process. A head collar allows you to turn a dog's head gently away from a stimulus that is causing concern, which in turn quietens the dog. The dog quickly learns he has the option to look away from a perceived threat and as his body language develops and expands, he becomes more confident and therefore less defensive.

After we went through some leash work, showing Sarah how to stay up by Sam's shoulder and walking him in an

Sam became more and more relaxed…

…and allowed Sarah to work around his mouth and on his beard

Introducing a head collar and changing Sarah's leading position greatly improved Sam's focus and balance

S-shape, Sam stopped pulling and no longer needed to keep rushing back to Sarah's partner for reassurance.

One of the most striking changes was the silence. Instead of staring intently and barking at anything that moved in his direct eye line, Sam was able to look quietly and calmly around the garden. The constant need to be active was replaced by a serene contentment and Sam was sitting and enjoying his surroundings.

Sam still has a long way to go but the alterations that we saw in his behaviour in those two days are extremely promising. Sarah has learned many new techniques to help her dog and the beauty of it is that she brought about all the changes herself. TTouch offers choices, and choices offer hope. As so many behaviours are linked, it doesn't take hours to work through and alter a dog's responses to individual situations. All that is required is understanding, patience and the desire to make a difference to an animal's life.

From Sarah Whiffen's perspective

During two sessions on consecutive days working with Sam under Sarah's guidance, I was definitely able to help him. If I hadn't both seen and felt the changes in his body under my own inexperienced hands, I wouldn't have believed such an overnight difference to be possible. I was able to work on areas

Sam was able to sit and take in his surroundings. He calmly watched a flock of birds flying overhead and stopped barking at anything that moved in his eyeline

Sarah was able to work on parts of Sam's body that he wouldn't usually let her touch

At the end of the session Sam actually sat on his right hip – for at least two and a half years his habitual pattern had been to sit on his left hip

of Sam's body he won't usually allow me to touch. His posture and demeanour relaxed, and all signs of anxiety left his eyes. For the first time in two and a half years, he was able to sit with his weight on his right rather than his left hip.

After the second early morning session, Sam spent the rest of the day quiet and contented without any of his usual frantic activity. A few days on and his reactions to a variety of situations have been less intense than before. Sam even allowed a repairman into our home without too much fuss!

Sam used to be unable to eat his food unless he had a member of our family standing with him, but after his TTouch sessions he was suddenly able to eat his dinner without being watched. A spike of hair on his back in an area where I've continued to work at home has started to lie flat. Sam settles immediately when he wears his calming band, much to the amazement of family members, and he demands daily TTouch sessions. I can now work around his beard and inside his mouth. We have had visitors with children staying for the past week and Sam behaved perfectly – the kids loved him and he had a great time playing with them and being adored so we are very proud of him. Ha! We are all feeling very hopeful and inspired.

The ribs, barrel and flanks

This area is often neglected. However, stomach problems can be associated with separation anxiety, clingy behaviour, gut imbalance, worry and sensitivity. Tension in this area can also be caused by problems in the back, which can trigger digestive disturbances. The colour of the belly can give you information about the dog's stress levels as hyperactive dogs or those that suffer from an allergy will tend to have pink or red skin that may be hot to the touch.

Dogs that carry tension through the ribs, flanks and stomach may dislike being picked up, may find towel drying uncomfortable and may react to wearing a harness. They may also dislike having their front or hind limbs picked up and may favour lying on one side when resting. The end of the ribcage, towards the tail, can be a sensitive

Indicators of tension through the ribs, barrel and flanks

Dogs that have tension through the ribs, barrel and flanks may also:

- Carry tension through the shoulders and inside hind leg
- Be jealous and overly protective
- Be slow to gain weight or drop weight easily
- Lack focus
- Have obsessive, compulsive behaviours
- Exhibit overly submissive behaviours

Tension in the ribs and belly can be linked to dogs that are over the top and clingy

This dog is very one-sided and habitually stands with a curve through his body

Not surprisingly he is sensitive to contact around the back of the ribs

Working around the ribcage will help to release the barrel and the back and improve his posture

area for some dogs and may trigger reactive behaviours when the animal is touched in this area. Dogs that are in a constant state of stress may have a dry coat on either side of their ribs and flanks. They may be noise-sensitive and pant or drool. They may dislike contact along the midline and may find it hard to soften and lengthen the topline. Tension through the ribs is often linked to tension in the back and can limit the dog's ability to flex and move in an arc or bend in a specific direction.

The hindquarters and tail

Tension in the hindquarters is common in dogs that lack confidence. They can be extremely noise-sensitive and find travelling in cars or standing on a raised platform, such as the grooming table, difficult as the ability to balance is impaired through tension in the hip and pelvis area. Hip displasia and arthritis can be linked to this pattern and can lower the dog's tolerance to everyday situations. Tension in the lower back and hindquarters can trigger the flight/fight reflex. If tension occurs elsewhere in the back, the dog may develop a dip just above the tail where the hair is raised.

Allergies or inappropriate food can result in sensitive hindquarters and are often present in dogs with over-the-top behaviours. Dogs that are habitually reactive to people and/or other dogs are often straight through the stifle. Even though this posture is often linked to the dog's inherent conformation, bodywork and groundwork can help increase mobility in the hindquarters as well as reducing the effect this posture has on the rest of the body.

Tail carriage

A constantly wagging tail does not necessarily indicate a happy dog. It can be caused by tension through the back and hindquarters and often accompanies vocal, nervous or excitable behaviour. If the base of the tail is tight, it can impair a dog's ability to sit. The dog may prefer

Dogs that carry tension through the hindquarters may be reluctant to travel in a car

They may also be concerned about contact around their tail

A high-set tail is often accompanied by a high head-carriage

to stand and stay or sit on one hip keeping the tail free. Dogs with docked tails can be tight through the pelvis and 'hop' behind. Sitting may be impossible due to the length of the remaining tail.

A high-set tail generally accompanies a high head-carriage and tight or straight back (see The back, p.64). It can be linked to dogs that are quick to arousal and over-reactive in their behaviour to people and other dogs, although dogs with this natural posture and conformation can also have a more passive nature and socialize easily with people and dogs. Contrary to some beliefs, it is not always the sign of a 'dominant' dog.

A tail that is tucked between the legs is an indication of a fearful dog. He may be a fear biter and have tendency to nip once and then retreat. The expression 'to tuck your tail and run' can be applied to dogs and those that are habitually tucked in the tail are often also in the flight reflex. They may find it hard to walk in a straight line and will often 'hug' the ground when walking on a leash, curving their body and leaning away from the handler.

Indicators of tension in the hindquarters and tail

Dogs that are tight in the hindquarters and tail may also:

- Be reluctant to get into a car
- Find it hard to relax when in a car
- Be worried by thunder, fireworks, ringing telephones, washing machines and so on
- React to strange dogs or people
- Be worried about movement behind them
- Have cold feet and cold ear tips
- Like to den and hide under tables, chairs, beds and so on
- Be reluctant to mate
- Dislike having their temperature checked
- Urinate through fear when approached

Some dogs have exceptionally floppy tails. Although this may seem to be an indicator of relaxation, it can be a sign of an aloof, shut-down or disinterested dog, or a dog that has tension through the middle of the back and/or the pelvis.

There is a correlation between the back and the tail. The base of the tail represents the base of the neck and shoulders, the middle of the tail represents the middle of the back and the end of the tailbone is linked to the pelvis. If a dog moves on the forehand he is likely to be tight at the base of the tail. If the dog is disconnected through the hindquarters, the end of the tailbone may feel as though it is separate from the rest of the tail. If the pelvis drops to one side, the end of the tailbone will often tilt in that direction. If an injury is present in the spine there is often a 'holding' through the corresponding vertebrae in the tail. By working slowly and mindfully with the tail it is possible to improve both gait and behaviour.

The feet

Lower legs and pads that feel cold can indicate nervousness. When a person is worried about a situation they may say 'I have cold feet about it'. The same applies to dogs.

Cool paws can also be a sign that circulation to the lower leg and feet is impaired and can be linked to tension in the shoulder and /or hindquarters. This may lead to problems with nail clipping, due not only to sensitivity in the paws, but also the dog's inability to balance on three legs. It can also be linked to travelling issues and reluctance to stand on tables for grooming or judging or to work over agility equipment as the dog may feel unsafe on a raised surface or on something that moves beneath his feet.

Splayed toes may be due to an injury but they can also tell you how your dog is distributing his weight through his limbs. Scuffed nails, and flatter, rounder, shinier pads indicate an uneven posture.

Chili was born with deformed feet. Note how the shape of his pads are linked to the shape of his feet and toes

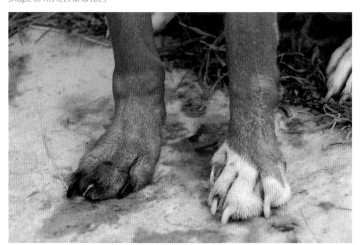

Indicators of tension in the feet

Dogs that have tension around their feet may also:
- Be worried about walking over different textures
- Dislike walking through water or on wet grass
- Be nervous about being picked up
- Be noise-sensitive
- Nibble their feet
- Bite through fear
- Have compulsive behaviours
- Have a dry coat or large areas where the coat is poor

TAKING STEPS TO HELP YOUR DOG

If your own dog has some of the tension patterns described in 'Assessing your Dog', you can take positive steps to improve them using TTouch techniques. TTouch has helped thousands of dogs overcome health and behavioural issues by using bodywork and groundwork exercises to change existing habitual patterns. The dogs learn to learn. They become calmer, more focused, easier to train and more adaptive to new situations. To paraphrase Oliver Wendell Holmes, 'A mind that has been expanded by new experiences cannot go back to its old dimensions.'

Training and behaviour

Training a dog does not only occur when he goes to a training class; when we use a clicker or a whistle, pick up the treat bag or put a leash on our dog – every time we interact with him, we are teaching him something, whether we are aware of it or not. Dogs are affected by stress and are thrown by inconsistency. They learn from experiences, both positive and negative, and from the people and animals around them. Your own reactions to the world around you will have a huge influence on how your dog responds to stimuli.

Understanding your dog

It can be very easy to jump to the wrong conclusions when trying to understand dog behaviour. If, for example, a rescue dog 'goes bananas' when he sees a person wearing a cap, the new owner might think that the dog has a history of being mistreated by someone who wore a hat. This may, in fact, not necessarily be true. Animals are far more visually aware than humans. A hat changes the shape of a person, and it may be that the dog is unable to place and understand the outline he sees. Tension in the upper part of the neck can also affect the way a dog processes visual information, as can the set of the eye. By reducing tension through the neck, improving body awareness and increasing the dog's self-carriage through bodywork and groundwork exercises, you can help him learn self-confidence and self-control. You can also use the groundwork exercises to introduce new shapes to the dog, regardless of his age, expanding his experience in a positive way.

Enjoying your dog

If your dog is living with more than one person, you must establish what each person finds acceptable in terms of dog behaviour. Some people do not mind if the dog sits or sleeps on the furniture or jumps up to greet them when they arrive home. For others these behaviours are a no-no. It can confuse the dog if members of the household have a different expectation of how a dog should act. Personally, I do not mind if my dogs sleep on the couch. Equally, I do not find that I must always be the person to walk through the door first to prevent them from ruling the roost – if my dog needs to go into the garden in the middle of the night during a howling gale because he has a tummy upset, I am more than willing to let him exit the kitchen on his own. I live in a multi-dog household and have never had a problem with any of my dogs thinking they have the upper hand, because I expect them to be able to function as a social member of a group and I listen to their needs.

It is important, however, that every dog learns simple obedience such as sit, stay, off, leave, wait, come and so on. If these basic commands are not in place from an early age, problems may arise as the dog matures. You can use a whistle and a clicker to establish good recall in your own home before you even venture out into the park. Learn as much as you can about the different developmental stages of dogs. Many dogs begin to ignore their owners around the age of one, even if basic training is in place from an early age. This is natural and can be easily overcome with understanding and patience.

Muzzles

It is worth teaching any dog to accept a muzzle. You never know when you might need to rely on this equipment as even the most placid dogs can change dramatically if they are in pain and have to be examined by a vet. Use the exercises for introducing a calming band (p.100) to help your dog accept a muzzle, and use treats and a clicker to encourage your dog to put his nose inside the muzzle without concern. This work will dramatically reduce his anxiety should you need to muzzle him in an emergency.

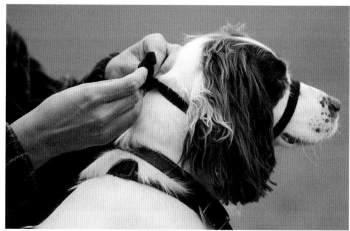

You can start training your dog to accept a muzzle by using a piece of simple sewing elastic to accustom him to the feeling of something around his head (for more information, see Face elastic p.100)

Travelling

Many owners often find that they do not actually need to work on specifics to overcome a problem when they use the TTouch techniques. For example, teaching your dog to walk over raised boards is often enough to help the dog overcome his fear of getting into a car.

Right: Sally finds it hard to get into a car (see p.71) partly because she has tension around the hindquarters. Tina teaches her to walk along a raised board and uses TTouches around her hindquarters. You can see from Sally's expression that she is nervous about contact on this part of her body

Far right: The change is dramatic. A few moments later Sally is confident to walk up the ramp, along the walk-over board and into the car

She sits quietly in the car and Tina gives her a treat

The walk-over board is left in place to help Sally get out of the car

She jumps in and out several times. Getting in and out of the car has now become easy and fun

Positive v. negative

When you are interacting with a dog, focus on what you want him to do rather than what you don't want him to do. Give him boundaries that are acceptable, achievable, maintainable and above all fair. If you are trying to teach a dog to change a habit, you may have to change your own reactions and responses first. This is not as easy as it sounds, but it will give you a greater understanding of how habit-based we all are. It is a definition of madness to do the same action over and over and expect a different outcome.

Many people have a strong idea of how they want their dog to behave but when asked what they actually want from their dog, their response is usually to describe the behaviour that they want to stop. For example, if they live with a dog that pulls when out and barks excessively in the house and/or the car, they will probably say, 'I want my dog to stop being so noisy and to stop dragging me down the street.' This way, they hold in their mind the image of the dog performing all the unwanted behaviours. Feel the difference when this train of thought is voiced positively, 'I would like my dog to walk calmly by my side and to be relaxed and quiet in the home and/or the car'. This creates a totally different image and someone saying this would automatically feel more positive that a successful resolution is achievable.

Reactive behaviour towards dogs and people

If your dog has serious issues around other dogs or people you must seek the advice of a professional who can help you on a one-to-one basis. As an owner you are wholly responsible for the way your dog behaves in society. TTouch can still form an integral part of the rehabilitation process as it reduces stress and will give you tools to help influence arousal levels before they escalate beyond your control.

If a dog is reactive to other dogs, many TTouch practitioners work with fake dogs as part of the training programme. Dogs read shape and outline far more than they use their nose. It can be quite enlightening to watch a dog's responses to a stuffed toy. The majority will respond in exactly the same way that they would if they were meeting a real dog. A fake dog can be 'walked' on a harness to simulate a moving animal. This can help an owner understand how fearful their dog is when he comes across another canine and can increase a dog's levels of self-confidence and self-control as the fake dog will obviously remain neutral at all times.

A fake dog can be the perfect first step to helping dogs overcome their concerns around other canines

Sudden behavioural changes

If your dog suddenly changes his behaviour there is likely to be an underlying cause. This may require veterinary attention or a referral from your vet for the dog to have holistic support such as acupuncture, homeopathy, McTimoney, cranio-sacral therapy, hydrotherapy, and so on. By using the observations made in 'Assess your Dog' (pp.40–73), you will be able to look for potential causes and where necessary make appropriate changes to the management of the dog. You can use the bodywork and groundwork to change the dog's expectation, or to alter a negative association with a particular stimulus by influencing the nervous system in a positive way.

Training methods

Dogs, like humans, work on a motive and reward basis. (Robin E. Walker BVetMed MRCVS is an inspirational and thought-provoking lecturer on the subject of reward chemistry and if you ever have the opportunity to hear him speak you will gain invaluable insights as to why behavioural problems can develop.) Training at any level and at any age should enhance the relationship between the dog and his handler or owner. Above all it should be fun for all concerned. Sadly there are still advocates of punishment and negative reinforcement. There really is no excuse for opting for methods that rely on pain or fear. They are not only cruel but also often ineffective, as fear and pain inhibit the ability for any being to learn. Harsh techniques, such as hanging or hitting a dog when a handler perceives him as doing something wrong, can also trigger more reactive responses, and make the situation escalate to dangerous proportions.

If a dog won't do something it is usually because he can't, because he is sore or afraid, because he doesn't understand what is being asked of him, is receiving mixed messages or because there isn't a motive or a high enough reward for him to change what he is doing. Addressing the source of the problem, with professional help if necessary, rather then merely trying to interrupt the behaviour is far more appropriate and far more effective.

Selecting a trainer or training method

Picking a trainer and training method for your dog is as important as all other aspects of canine care. Remember you can't change the past but you can shape the future.

If you are watching a video, a demonstration, a television programme, a training class or a private session, ask yourself the following questions to see whether a particular approach is appropriate for you:

- Are what the trainer says and what the trainer does the same?
- If you could put yourself in the dog's position how would you feel, and what would you be learning from the experience?
- How do you truly feel in your gut and in your heart when you watch the dog being worked or handled?
- Could you do the same?
- Does the dog look as though he is enjoying the experience?
- What does the trainer do when what they are doing or asking the dog to do doesn't work? Do they have alternative ideas and try another approach, do they make the lesson easier for the dog to understand, do they give the dog a break, or play a game? Or do they punish the dog and escalate their own behaviour doing more of the same but harder?

If you are watching the trainer on a video, DVD or television programme, try turning the sound down; at a demonstration try watching the trainer in action with your ears covered. It can be quite enlightening to watch the dog's expressions and responses without being distracted by words and sounds.

The exercises – bodywork and groundwork

Bodywork (specific, passive movements of the skin, legs, tail and ears) can be used to release tension, reduce stiffness, improve circulation, increase body awareness and improve mobility and performance. It can enable dogs to overcome a fear of contact, change an expectation or memory of pain, and helps dogs to be easier to handle and train. Bodywork also helps to trigger the parasympathetic nervous system (p.14), encourages deep and rhythmical breathing, which boosts the immune system, improves sensory integration, reduces stress, improves performance and promotes a sense of wellbeing in the dog. It also helps to develop a unique and deep rapport between the dog and his owner/handler.

Groundwork (slow, considered movements on the leash) helps the dog to develop flexibility and balance. It establishes a solid foundation for all training and competitive work as the dog learns true self-carriage. It enables the dog to learn how to move his body in a more effective way without placing unnecessary stress on one particular joint or joints. It also releases tension, teaches focus and obedience and improves co-ordination. Groundwork enables the dog to become active rather than simply reactive.

Ten minutes of groundwork can be far more beneficial for shelter dogs or those with limited access to exercise than 20 minutes hurtling around off lead, which can actually make excitable behaviours worse. Dogs that are too stressed to tolerate being touched can go on to be successfully rehabilitated when taught groundwork. After one or two sessions working over poles (pp.115 and 121) and different surfaces (p.120), the changes in posture and behaviour are often so significant that bodywork can then be safely introduced. The time span in which this happens will obviously vary from dog to dog.

Belle by *Fiona Habershon*

Belle, a three-year-old Saluki x Pointer, is a rescue dog, known to have been brought up in a travellers' camp. The first thing that I noticed about her when she came to live with me was that she would not give eye contact to anyone and if you moved your hand she would immediately cringe as if she was expecting to be hit. Her tail was always clamped between her hind legs and she kept her head low. She would allow me to touch her but was always pulling away, ready to escape. You could feel her fear.

I was studying to become an animal behaviourist and dog trainer and knew I had to get her eye contact before I was ever going to be able to start any form of training with her. I had to gain Belle's trust. Although over the months our relationship had grown, I was still getting very little eye contact. I knew there was something missing.

I then came across an article about the Tellington TTouch and the more I researched the more I could see how it would fit in seamlessly with the other work I was training to do, so I decided to become a practitioner.

Once I had completed two workshops I felt confident enough to try TTouch work on Belle and BANG – breakthrough! after just one short session she gave me a direct look. Each day I would do three 5–10 minute sessions and the eye contact became longer and longer. She started to listen to me and after only two weeks her recall had dramatically improved and she no longer cringed or shied away.

The bond that has now developed between the two of us is indescribable. TTouch has created a way for us to communicate with each other that is far beyond the standard routes of training.

Special considerations

The exercises in this book are suitable for all dogs of all ages, sizes and builds. However, be careful to tailor the sessions to suit the dog and always be aware of how the dog is feeling. Don't persist with something if it is causing concern.

- **Puppies**
  Puppies have a short concentration span and tire easily. Work little and often and keep the sessions varied and fun.

- Teach the puppy containment by sitting on your heels on the floor and placing the puppy between your thighs. Support him gently around his chest with his head facing away from you and use your palms lightly to move the skin over his shoulders. While maintaining the support with one hand, use your other hand to work lightly around his chest, up his neck, over his head and around his muzzle and face.

Give the puppy plenty of breaks and allow him time to play

Teaching a puppy containment is best done in short sessions interspersed with TTouch work, clicker training and play

Work all over the puppy's body, including his feet

- If the puppy is concerned, work for 30 seconds or so and then let him go. Repeat this exercise a few times and intersperse it with a little clicker training, groundwork and/or games. If the puppy is enjoying the bodywork, you can work all over his body including his feet, but the session should still be short. Mouthing is a natural puppy response but hard or frantic biting accompanied by growling or screaming is a sign that your puppy has concerns. If he wriggles around go with his movement without pinning or restraining him. If the situation does not improve quickly consult a TTouch practitioner who can work with you on a one-to-one basis.

Use your fingertips to work gently around the puppy's mouth and gums

- Groundwork adds variety to leash work and can be mentally stimulating for a young pup. Teaching pups to walk over different surfaces and negotiate ramps is an important part of their development.

- **Children and dogs**

  Teaching children how to do some simple TTouches such as the Clouded Leopard or Chimp TTouch (pp.95–97) can give them gentle ways of interacting with their animals. TTouch teaches children to be more considered and more appropriate in their approach and to respect dogs. It helps them to be more thoughtful and also improves a child's dexterity and self-control.

Teaching puppies to walk over different surfaces is an important part of their development

TTouch gives children gentle, appropriate ways of interacting with their animals

Jenna is really enjoying the ear slides that Ben has learnt

Special considerations (continued)

- **Older dogs**
  The majority of the exercises in this section can help keep your old friend happy and active during his twilight years. Raised poles may not be appropriate for dogs that have joint problems but other groundwork exercises, such as the labyrinth (p.118), can play a vital role in maintaining good balance and proprioception. They can keep an older dog mentally stimulated without placing excessive strain on his heart and body and can help him adjust to a change in routine if his exercise has to be reduced.

- Some dogs can become more sensitive to hand contact as their muscle tone changes. A sheepskin mitt, more generally used for grooming horses can be used when doing the TTouches (p.95). Circling the legs (p.109) is probably best done while the dog is lying down to prevent him from falling or becoming uncomfortable.

- You can also learn some acupressure techniques (p.91) to help settle an old dog that may start showing signs of anxiety as he ages, particularly if you have to move house or there is a change in the household such as the arrival of a younger dog or baby. In contrast to its name, you only need to rest your fingertips lightly on the points to improve the flow of Qi.

A few minutes of TTouch everyday enables you to check for any changes and gives you one-to-one time together

Groundwork is invaluable for older dogs or those that are on reduced exercise

KEY SKILLS

Leash work, exercises for balance, proprioception and sensory integration, the half body wrap and TTouches are key skills that any dog and owner will benefit from learning for use everyday. They are described over the next few pages.

Leash work

A high proportion of dogs have problems when on a leash. They may pull, spin, leap in the air, walk on their hind legs and/or may become more agitated when faced with something that concerns them.

Dogs pull or escalate their behaviour when on a leash largely because of the effect that the lead has upon their balance.

A single lead and flat collar can trigger pulling

When pressure is applied to a collar, the balance of the dog is changed – here it is pulled onto the left hind limb

An example of a two-point contact using a head collar and a flat collar

Physical balance, emotional balance and mental balance are linked. On the lead, most dogs are taught to stop through a signal on the neck rather than by learning how to halt or slow down through their bodies, so they have not learned how to move their centre of gravity backwards. As dogs carry most of their weight over the front limbs, there is a natural tendency for a dog to pull as he is already moving on the forehand. In addition, leading a dog purely from a flat collar can have a detrimental effect on his body. When pressure is applied to the collar, the weight distribution through the body will be uneven and the hip nearest the handler will often bear more of the load. Over time this could present a problem for the dog, as the muscle development will be uneven.

Dogs can also become more frustrated on a lead because their option to flee is prevented, and pressure on the collar causes bracing through the neck, shoulders, withers and back, which in turn triggers more defensive reactions. Fortunately there are several ways to help dogs overcome any difficulties they have with lead work without the need for harsh techniques.

Two-point contact

TTouch leading techniques improve proprioception and balance and so can dramatically improve both the posture and the behaviour of the dog. Teaching a dog to walk calmly on a leash using two-point contact – the handler having two distinct connections with the dog, usually with a double-ended leash – can have a miraculous and often instantaneous effect. There are many ways of using two-point contact, so this leading technique can be easily tailored to suit the individual dog's needs. The exercises will also help to reduce tension in the handler's shoulders and back and do not require years of experience to be effective.

Teaching a dog to walk using two-point contact can have a miraculous and instantaneous effect

TTouch leash work teaches a dog how to respond to the signals given by his handler in a way that does not upset him physically or emotionally. Teaching a dog to walk with a harness and flat collar combination is also beneficial from a safety point of view. If your dog becomes scared or suddenly runs backwards there is less risk of him slipping out of the equipment. It also means that a slip collar, or a tightly fitted flat collar is not the only option for a dog whose neck is wider than his head.

A flat collar and lead encourages Jess to pull her handler along

Teaching a dog to walk with a harness and flat collar helps to reduce pulling, and improves both posture and behaviour

Choosing an appropriate combination

The possible two-point combinations are:
- **Head collar and flat collar**
- **Head collar and harness**
- **Flat collar and harness**
- **Harness with the lead attached to two points on the harness**
- **Rope harness and flat collar**

To work out which is the best combination for your dog, ask yourself what you would like to achieve and really look at how your dog moves when walking on a lead.

- If your dog fixates on cars, objects, people and/or other animals, it might be worth introducing a head collar and harness combination so that you can teach him to turn away from any stimulus that gives him cause for concern.
- If your dog leans into his existing collar or you find you have to continually check him back, a flat collar and harness combination or attaching the lead to two points of contact on the harness may be more appropriate.

Jess – head collar and harness

Handler posture

Regardless of the equipment used, another important factor when leading a dog is the balance, position and body awareness of the handler. It takes two to maintain a pull. If the handler is bracing through their body, is behind the dog's shoulder or is totally out of balance, the dog will tighten and hold through his own body and will probably pull more. It will also be harder for the handler to influence the posture of the dog and any attempt to do so could result in a sharp correction rather than a fluid, easy movement that the dog can process and understand. A dog will take his cue to move or respond to stimulus from the handler and will be influenced by the movement and direction of the handler's shoulders, hips, hands and feet. Learning to stay up by your dog's shoulders can help you give visual information to your dog.

Hand position on the lead is also important. A tight grip on the lead will tighten the handler's shoulders and create more of a pull on the lead. For every action, there is an equal and opposite reaction: the dog will compensate for the constant pressure on the lead by pulling away more and it will be hard to distinguish who is walking whom. Holding the lead across the palm of your hand with the fingers relaxed and on top of the lead as opposed to underneath it, will enable you to be subtler with the signals. Holding the lead in this manner will soften your arms, shoulders and back, reducing the risk of injury to both parties if the dog suddenly lunges or leaps in the air.

Walking up by the dog's shoulder enables you to be more fluid in your movement and allows you to influence the dog rather than simply correcting him

If the handler is bracing or is behind the dog, the dog will tighten and brace through his shoulders

Stroking the lead

If your dog is generally impeccably behaved on the lead but occasionally roots or freezes, or if a flat collar is your only option, you can stroke the lead to encourage him to move or turn. Ideally, you need to be up by his shoulder for this to be totally effective, but if you have slipped back by mistake you can use the technique to slow him down so that you can reposition yourself. It is highly effective and far nicer for the dog if this method is employed instead of the common check-and-release technique.

- Stand parallel to the dog's shoulder with your body angled slightly away from him. Ensure that there is enough distance between you to allow the dog to turn. Slightly soften your knees, hips and shoulders. If you brace it will not have the same effect.

Stroking the lead can encourage a dog to move if he has gone into freeze (see p.18). It removes the need to pull on the collar and helps the handler to stay mobile through their own shoulders

- Hold the lead in both hands with your hands about 20–30cm (8–12in) apart. Take up a contact on the lead so that you connect with the dog but make sure that you are not pulling on the lead.

- Starting with the hand furthest away from you, draw it along the lead towards the other hand maintaining an even contact on the lead. Stroke the lead slowly and gently with alternate hands by moving one hand over the top of the other hand until the dog steps towards you. Look in the direction that you want to go.

- Be patient and refrain from escalating the movement if the dog doesn't respond immediately. The aim is to draw the dog towards you or to ask him to move forwards, rather than to reel him in, so make sure that your hands aren't creeping up the lead by mistake. You can use your voice to encourage him and to praise him the moment he looks or turns in your direction so that he understands exactly what is being asked of him.

• Keep stroking the lead and asking the dog to move. If you are wanting him to walk forward, ask for a few paces and then praise him and ask again. You can walk him through the labyrinth (p.118) or over poles laid on the ground (pp.110, 112) so that he has something else to focus on. If the labyrinth is too much, walk him between two poles laid together on the ground. You can also use a clicker to click each time he steps forward if you are confident with clicker training (see p.26).

You can also stroke the lead to maintain a constant connection with your dog if you are:

• Waiting at the vet
• Standing chatting in the park or outside the shops
• Steadying the dog if he is moving quickly forward to greet another friend
• In a training class
• Outside the show ring or in the show ring

This technique originated with TTouch work with horses (TTEAM). The beauty of working with different animal species is being able to experiment with the application of the various methods. I introduced stroking the lead to the dog work while teaching at Battersea and the results were truly astonishing. Dogs that were so strong they were almost pulling the handler over, not only relaxed and softened through their body, but also became more focused and quieter.

Recently my editor, Jo Weeks, told me how this technique had worked like a dream with one of her dogs who always resists being brought to the hosepipe for a rinse off after a muddy walk. Although Border Collie Lucy doesn't particularly mind being hosed down, she hates to be pulled about on the lead. While Lucy was straining on the lead hoping to avoid a wash, Jo remembered what she had read in my draft manuscript the day before. She decided to stroke the lead to see what happened. She got a surprise – Lucy softened her whole body and turned to face her within a couple of seconds, soon moving back towards her and the tap. Jo knows about TTouch techniques and has tried them with success before, but it didn't prevent her from being amazed at how quickly this technique produced a result.

The act of stroking the lead has a profound effect and when this technique is demonstrated on people who hold one end of the lead in their hands, they are startled at the powerful sensation they experience through their entire body. Even with their eyes closed they feel an overwhelming desire to move towards the person stroking the other end of the line.

My dog doesn't like stroking the lead

If your dog remains rooted, backs away or looks confused, check the following:

• Make sure you are not pulling on the collar. The aim is to soften the dog's neck so that he releases through the shoulders and ribs
• Try slowing the movement down – you may be working too quickly
• Make sure you aren't bracing or tense through any part of your body
• Look in the direction that you want to go and ensure you aren't staring at the dog, standing too close or standing square on
• Make sure you are maintaining a gentle and even contact on the lead – if the movement is too passive the dog will not be able to feel the signals
• Make sure you aren't confusing the dog with too many voice commands

Balance leash

This is a quick and simple way of helping to reduce pulling if you only have a flat collar on your dog. It will not work if you have one short lead. If you do not have a long lead, loop two leads together. The technique is particularly helpful for shelter dogs that are desperate to get out of their kennels and drag their handlers when going to the paddocks or out on a walk.

Balance leash work reduces tension on the neck and gives a signal on the chest, which helps to move the dog's centre of gravity backwards. It helps to instil balance and self-control, and can be used to teach a dog to sit quietly and patiently when other dogs may be moving around him, such as in training classes, at shows and at competitions.

- If the dog is on your left, support the lead in your left hand and drop the remainder of the length of the lead around the dog's left shoulder and across his chest with your right hand. You should now be holding the end of the lead in your right hand. (If your dog is on your right, you will drop the lead around his right shoulder and will be holding the end of the lead in the your left hand.)

- Give a slow ask-and-release signal: do this by giving a gentle signal backwards with both hands and then slowly melting, or softening, the contact. Repeat as necessary until the dog slows down. This will encourage your dog to walk quietly by your side. If you maintain a backwards pull he will simply lean into the leash. Most people find that this works immediately but if the dog leaps about, jumps over or backs out of the lead try the balance leash plus.

The ask-and-release signal across the chest teaches the dog to move his centre of gravity backwards which reduces pulling and removes pressure from the neck

Support the lead in your left hand and drop the lead around the dog's chest

My dog doesn't like the balance leash

- Check that the dog isn't sore across his chest
- Make sure that you are not keeping a constant pressure on the lead, which will trigger more of a pull
- Check your own posture, as bracing will make the dog lean more
- Try rotating your hips slowly from left to right as you walk. This will help to unlock the dog's shoulders and withers
- Make sure the loop in the lead hasn't risen up to the base of the dog's neck
- Do TTouch work (p.95) and lifts (pp.104, 107, 108) around the shoulders and chest
- Try using a half body wrap (p.93) at the same time

Balance leash plus

This is similar to the balance leash but with a simple addition. Instead of looping the lead around the chest, bring the lead between the dog's front legs – most dogs will actually step obligingly over the lead with their outside leg – then take it diagonally across his chest and thread it up through his collar. The end of the lead will still be in your outside hand (furthest from the dog) and your inside hand will still be holding the lead over the dog's back. Walk forward and if the dog starts to pull give a gentle ask-and-release with the hand that is holding the end of the lead. He should come back into balance straight away but if he doesn't, walk him a few paces at a time and stop. Keep the signals smooth and fluid. Praise him quietly when he is by your side so that he understands what is being asked of him. If he continues to lunge and pull, use this leading technique in conjunction with polework or weaving through cones (p.105) to improve his focus.

1 Loop the lead around the front of the dog, allowing the loop to drop to the ground

2 Most dogs will step over the lead with their outside leg and into the balance leash plus position

3 Take the lead diagonally across the chest and thread the end up through the collar

Leading the dog in a balance leash plus prevents the lead from rising up and putting pressure on the neck…

…and helps to reduce pulling and improve focus

Homing pigeon

Leading a dog between two people can help improve the dog's balance and is a useful way of accustoming the dog to be handled from his left side. It can be used to introduce a second person to the dog and has obvious benefits from a safety point of view. In addition it is helpful for:

- Dogs that spin, leap or lean
- Separation anxiety
- Reducing pulling
- Improving focus

- Attach a second lead or long line to any part of the harness or thread it through the opposite side of a flat collar, depending on the equipment already on the dog and the reason behind introducing a second handler. In order for this technique to be effective, the second lead must be attached to a separate point of contact. Never use two collars, as this will damage the dog's neck.

- Walk the dog between you through a labyrinth (p.118), over some poles (pp.110, 112, 115, 121) or other obstacle, or between some cones (see p.105).

A second lead can be added to any part of the harness or threaded through the collar. Make sure the second lead is not attached to the same point as the first lead

Acupressure

The aim of acupressure is to restore, replenish and maintain the natural harmony and balance needed by animals and humans to support optimal health and wellbeing. It offers you and your dog tools to influence natural healing and is a wonderful way to deepen the connection with your canine companion.

Yin Tang Point

This is especially useful for helping a dog with mental focus and calming. It can be used for the following issues: cognitive disorders, chronic restlessness, gaining attention for training. It is located on the midline of the head, slightly above the eyes (also known as the third eye).

Bai Hui

Traditionally called 'heaven's gate', dogs love a good scratching on this point. It generates energy along the spine and down the hindlegs, thus it is good for any hindquarter issues. Additionally, Bai Hui is a calming point, often used to support a dog's feeling of general wellbeing. It is located on the midline of the sacrum, where you can't feel the spinous processes.

Yang Tang Point

This relieves worry, disperses anxiety and is helpful for dogs with Canine Compulsive Disorders (CCD), such as repetitive licking or chewing of paws, barking constantly, over-eating or not eating, all indicators of high levels of stress. It is located approximately one finger's width beyond the outer canthus of the eye (angle where the upper and lower eyelid meet).

Governing vessel 20 (GV20)

The 'point of 100 meetings' has many attributes. It is known for its ability to calm the mind while also releasing heat from the body. Thus, it can be used for fevers, states of anger and aggression, as well as relieving anxiety and worry. It is located directly on the top of the dog's head, midway between the front edges of the ears. Placing the palm of your hand on this point can have a very calming effect on a dog.

It will probably be easier for the dog in the beginning if two-point contact is used when introducing the walk-over board

The walk-over board can help prepare a dog for using a ramp to get into a car, become accustomed to the vet's or judge's table and can also improve a dog's self-confidence

The teeter totter can help improve balance and is useful for dogs that are timid, over the top and/or concerned about travelling in a car

Exercises for balance, proprioception and sensory integration

While all the exercises in this section will help develop balance, proprioception and sensory integration in your dog, the walk-over board and the teeter totter (see saw) are more specifically designed to improve co-ordination, self-carriage and focus. It may be easier and more comfortable for the dog to lead him with two-point contact (see p.83) for these exercises as it will enable you to guide him over the obstacles more effectively.

Teeter totter

Teaching him to walk over a low-level teeter totter can help a timid dog and one with concerns about travelling in the car. It can provide a foundation for agility work if the dog is nervous or young and is a great way to help a dog build confidence and learn self-control.

Walk-over board

The walk-over board can also help build confidence. A nervous dog may find it difficult to leave the ground when asked although he may happily jump onto a chair at home. This is a useful exercise to help a dog to feel safe when on a table at the vet or a show, or on a grooming table as some dogs will freeze when in these situations. You can ask the dog to stand in the middle of the board and do some TTouches all over his body to help him relax and to accustom him to being handled when on a raised surface.

Ask the dog to stand in the middle of the board while you do some TTouches on his body to help him relax and to teach him to feel more confident

The idea is to allow the dog to work out how to walk slowly and calmly over both the teeter totter and the walk-over board. Avoid luring a dog over or forcing him to stay on the boards if he panics, loses his balance or rushes. These exercises will also improve your handling skills.

My dog doesn't like raised surfaces

* Start with a simple board laid flat on the ground
* Lead him over different surfaces (p.120)
* Try a half body wrap (right) and/or bodywork to give him greater body awareness

Half body wrap

The TTouch half body wrap is a simple tool that helps to improve balance and co-ordination. It provides sensory information and increases awareness. It can be used for dogs that are worried by noise, or are unsettled when travelling in a car. It can help increase confidence and reduces over the top behaviours such as jumping up or excessive activity.

The half wrap is also a useful step in teaching dogs to wear a harness, including working dogs and service dogs. In addition it helps dogs that are:

* Clingy
* Jealous
* Worried by hand contact
* Concerned about being contained
* Nervous
* Tight in the shoulders
* Weak in the hindquarters

The wrap is made from a stretchy Ace medical bandage that comes in different sizes so you can purchase the appropriate width for your dog. (Ace bandages are available from the TTouch website, see p.127.) Crepe bandages are not as effective as they curl lengthwise.

The idea behind using the wrap is to provide sensory awareness rather than as a means of physically supporting or restraining the dog. The wrap must not be pulled tightly around the dog. Once it is on (see instructions overleaf), walk your dog on the lead or encourage him to move by playing a game.

* If your dog is worried about the wrap, to begin with simply stroke it gently against his side or do some circular TTouches with the wrap in your hand.

The half body wrap

Place the middle of the wrap gently across the dog's chest

Bring both ends up and over the shoulders crossing the wrap over the withers

Cross the wrap under the ribs and fasten on one side of the body. Make sure the knot or pin isn't sitting on the spine

- If the dog is happy, place the middle of the wrap across his chest and bring it up and over the top of his shoulders. Cross the wrap over his withers and take it round the ribs and under his sternum. Cross the wrap under the dog and bring both ends up over the ribcage. Pin the wrap or tie the ends in a bow or a quick-release knot. Make sure that the knot, pin or bow is off to one side of the spine and that the pin will not come undone. If your dog is worried by the sensation of the wrap crossing underneath his body, arrange the wrap in a figure of eight instead and fasten it by tying the ends in a bow – this way you can undo it quickly if the dog becomes concerned.

Only use the wrap for as long as the dog is concerned, that is for the duration of the fireworks or car journey. Never leave it on an unattended dog. Watch your dog's reactions and if he is worried stop immediately or remove the wrap instantly if he panics once it is on.

My dog doesn't like the half body wrap

- Check that it isn't too tight – there should be plenty of give left in the bandage
- Start by simply laying it over his shoulders
- Do bodywork around the chest (pp.106–110), shoulders and ribcage (pp.113–115)
- Try using a T-shirt or a dog coat instead

If your dog is worried by the wrap crossing under his ribs, fasten it in a simple figure of eight instead

TTouches

The various TTouches that make up part of the TTEAM technique break down into three groups: circles, slides and lifts. The TTouches often have a dramatic effect on animals and can elicit profound changes. They can be done anywhere on the dog's body and can teach a dog to accept and enjoy contact. When used on the dog's face they help to increase trust, release tight facial muscles, reduce barking and accustom a dog to being handled around the head or wearing a head collar.

When used on the body the TTouches help to:

- Increase circulation
- Reduce stiffness
- Promote a sense of calm and relaxation
- Increase self-confidence
- Release tension
- Change a dog's expectation of what hand contact might mean

Gemma is nervous of strangers and bites if touched on her body

After using groundwork and a fake hand (p.31) Tina is able to work on Gemma's body without causing her any distress

Pressure levels

The TTouch works on the nervous system and therefore requires relatively little pressure to be effective. To convey a sense of the amount of pressure that is appropriate when doing the TTouches, TTEAM uses a system of numbers from one to ten.

- **One pressure** Place your thumb lightly on your cheek and gently rest your fingertips on your cheekbone. With as light a pressure as possible move the skin over your cheekbone without rubbing so that you can barely feel the bone underneath your fingers. This is a one pressure. Practise by using the same pressure to move the skin on your forearm, noting that there is no indentation on the skin.

- **Three pressure** Moving the skin over the cheekbone with a little more pressure so that you can just feel the bone underneath your fingers gives you a three pressure. When using a three pressure on the forearm you should notice a slight indentation.

- **Six pressure** Doubling the three pressure gives a six pressure. Clouded Leopard TTouches are most commonly used with a pressure ranging from two to three depending on the preference of the dog and the area on which you are working.

TTouches can be done anywhere on a dog's body

Circular TTouches

Clouded Leopard TTouch is the foundation for all the circular TTouches. You can do the Clouded Leopard TTouch over the whole dog, altering your hand position where necessary around the contours of the body to ensure the movement remains fluid and relaxed.

- Visualize a clock face on the dog's body approximately 1cm (½in) in diameter with six o'clock being the lowest point. With one hand

The Clouded Leopard TTouch is the most commonly used TTouch

lightly holding the lead, supporting the collar, or resting on the dog's body, place the fingers of your other hand at six on your imaginary watch face. With your fingers in a softly curved position, like a paw, push the skin around the clock in a clockwise circle. Maintain an even pressure all the way round, on past six until you reach eight. At eight, pause for a second and if the dog is relaxed move to another spot and repeat the movement.

- It is important to make only one circular movement each time on any one spot and to ensure that your fingers are pushing the skin in a circle rather than sliding over the hair. When you make a circle rest your thumb lightly against the body to steady the hand. Move your first, second and third fingers as one to ensure that the little finger 'goes along for the ride'. If you tense the joints in your fingers or wrist the whole movement will become stiff. Allow your fingers to relax and move in the rotation.

- Practise doing the circular movements on the back of your hand to help soften your hands and give you a sense of how the TTouch differs from other bodywork. It is important to make sure your circles are really round and that they are made in one smooth, flowing movement.

- As you work, remember to breathe. Concentration can cause us to hold our breath, which stiffens our body and affects the TTouch.

The Raccoon TTouch can be done along either side of the spine

• **Raccoon TTouch** is excellent for working around the base of the ear, the base of the tail, along either side of the spine and around the back of the shoulder. You can also use it between the toes and around the nail beds as part of the steps to helping dogs overcome concerns with nail trimming.

The Raccoon TTouch can be used for working the area around wounds to speed up healing and to increase circulation and activate neural impulses in the lower legs. It is also used to reduce swelling without causing pain.

This TTouch is named after the tiny, delicate movements of a raccoon washing its food. From the Clouded Leopard position, curve your fingers more so that you are now making the circles with your fingertips, just behind the nails. Remember to keep your hand and fingers soft and allow movement through the knuckles.

• **Llama TTouch** suits nervous dogs or those that are protective about being touched on certain parts of their body as they may find contact with the back of the hand less threatening.

Keep your fingers soft and gently stroke the dog's muzzle and body with the back of your fingers. You can also try the circular movements with this TTouch.

• **Chimp TTouch** is particularly useful for nervous dogs. Make a soft open fist and use the area between the first and second joints on the back of the fingers to move the skin. Keep the fingers together and the hand soft.

TTouches that involve slides and lifts are described under the relevant exercises.

The Clouded Leopard TTouch is the most commonly used TTouch

The Llama TTouch is useful for nervous dogs or those that are protective about being touched on certain parts of the body

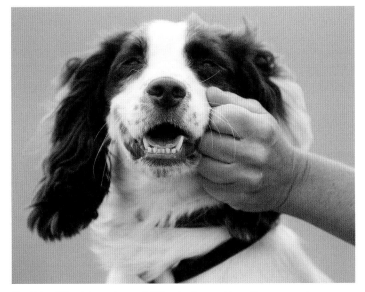

The Chimp TTouch is another useful TTouch when working with a nervous dog

My dog doesn't like circular TTouches

If your dog doesn't settle with the circular TTouches try:
- Lightening the pressure. Most people are amazed at how light this work is once they experience it on themselves
- Going in an anti-clockwise direction
- Lightly brushing your fingertips over the dog as though you were flicking dust from his face or body. If he settles add the occasional circle
- Speeding up or slowing down the movement
- Covering your hand with a sheepskin mitt (p.126)
- Using a different TTouch

WORKING ON SPECIFIC AREAS

The rest of this section focuses on exercises for particular areas of the body. Although they are specifically designed to help dogs with issues in those areas, they can also be used to reduce nervous, compulsive or over the top behaviours and they will improve any dog's sense of wellbeing.

THE MUZZLE

Mouth work

Accustoming a dog to be handled around the mouth is an important part of canine care. It enables you to carry out regular dental checks and will ensure that the dog remains calm during judging or vet examinations. Dogs that have issues around food or toys usually dislike contact around the muzzle. Mouth work can therefore form part of the rehabilitation process. In addition it is useful for:

- Dogs that are overly emotional and sensitive
- Reducing excessive barking or chewing
- Teething puppies
- Teaching a dog to release toys
- Improving trust
- Reducing reactive behaviours

Teaching a dog to be handled around the mouth is an important part of canine care

If the dog is nervous about being handled around the muzzle and jaw try using the Chimp TTouch

Support the dog's head with one hand and work gently around the lips

- Stand by the side of the dog's shoulder or sit on a chair with the dog facing away from you. If the dog turns round to face you stop immediately.

- Start by stroking the dog's muzzle and sides of the face with the back of your hand. If the dog is nervous you can start by using a different texture such as a soft paintbrush or sheepskin mitt, which may be less threatening.

- If the dog is happy, continue with the Chimp or Clouded Leopard TTouches (pp.96–97). Support the dog's head with your other hand. Work around the jaw muscles and move the upper lip in a circular motion. You can then slide a fingertip under the lip and rub it gently along the gum. Wet your fingers if the dog is dry in the mouth. If the dog is happy to be handled inside the mouth, work both gums. Switch hands and work the other side of the mouth.

Note: Do not persist with this type of exercise if you feel that your dog may nip. Get expert help to work through his problems.

Most dogs find mouth work very relaxing, but it can take several short sessions to get this effect if the dog is nervous or worried about being handled around the head

My dog doesn't like mouth work

- The mouth and tail are linked. If your dog is nervous of contact around the muzzle try working on the hindquarters and tail (pp.116–117)
- Make sure you are not gripping the head with your supporting hand
- Break the exercise down into easier steps and work in short sessions over several days
- Introduce him to a calming band or face elastic (p.100)

If the dog is happy, progress to working inside the mouth and slide a fingertip under the upper lip and work along the gum

Calming band/Face elastic

These work along the same lines as the half body wrap (p.93). The idea is not that they force the mouth to stay closed, or that the dog meets resistance from the bands when he barks and so tires. The aim is to enable the dog to become aware of himself, and to release tension through the muzzle. As a result the calming band or face elastic can quickly settle and quieten a hyperactive or excessively barking dog. They also help increase confidence and can encourage a dog to accept and enjoy contact around the face and mouth. In addition they are useful for:

- Dogs that are overly excited in the car
- Beginning to introduce a headcollar or muzzle
- Improving focus

A calming band can help the dog accept and enjoy contact around his head

- If your dog is happy to be handled around the head, do some TTouch work over the bridge of the nose and around the back of his head before popping on the calming band.

- Throw a ball for the dog, give him a treat or encourage him to walk so that he is comfortable and knows that his mouth movements are not inhibited in any way. If he slips the band off, do some TTouches and pop it back on again.

- If he dislikes contact around the mouth, try using the face elastic instead of the calming band. This may enable him to accept the contact more readily.

What are calming bands and face elastic?

Face elastic

This is made using a length of sewing elastic available from a haberdasher. Place the middle of the length of elastic over the dog's nose and cross the ends under the jaw. Bring the ends together on top of the neck and tie them in a bow behind the ears. Make sure that you do not pull the stretch from the elastic.

Calming band

This piece of equipment was developed from the face elastic. Calming bands are made from elastic and nylon webbing, are adjustable and come in different sizes and colours (they are available from the TTouch website, see p.127). The elastic part of the band is slipped on over the dog's nose. The nylon straps cross under the lower jaw and are fastened together behind the ears with a plastic clasp.

Take a length of soft sewing elastic and place it over the dog's nose. Cross it under the chin and tie the ends together in a bow behind his ears (see also p.76)

- Neither the calming band nor the face elastic should ever be forced on the dog, nor left on an unattended dog. They are tools to help dogs overcome a variety of issues and should be used in conjunction with other TTouch techniques to address the source of the problem rather than simply trying to control the behaviour.

A calming band is extremely beneficial for dogs that bark excessively…

…and usually brings immediate relief for all concerned

Molly is the perfect model for showing how useful the calming band can be for dogs that bark when in a car

She immediately settles and lies down. She can still open her mouth but is quiet and relaxed

My dog doesn't like the calming band/face elastic

- Check that he can eat properly and doesn't have dental or ear problems
- Start with a half body wrap (p.93)
- Work on his hindquarters and tail (pp.116–117)
- Try putting the face elastic over his forehead instead of over his nose

EYES, HEAD AND EARS

TTouch work

A hectic lifestyle and a noisy environment can cause stress in a dog, and gentle TTouch work around the eyes, head and ears can bring calm to both the handler and the dog. Try using Raccoon TTouches (p.97) around the jaw, around the base of the ears, around the ears and along the back of the skull. Use Clouded Leopard TTouches (p.96) across the head, working in connecting lines or at random, depending on the dog's responses. This work can be useful for:

- Quieting a barking dog
- Reducing behaviour before it escalates
- Helping a dog to sleep
- Concerns about being left alone
- Building trust and confidence and reducing instinctive responses

- If the dog is worried by contact on the head start by working on the neck or shoulders.

- Sit or stand next to your dog so that you are not facing him. Support his head with your other hand or hold his lead if you are outside to maintain a connection. Avoid putting your face too close to the dog and work slowly and gently over his whole head and face. Pay attention to any areas that may be giving him cause for concern.

- Several short sessions can be more beneficial than one long one. The length of a session will vary depending on the dog and why you are doing the work. Most TTouch practitioners use TTouches on their dog every day. Your dog will let you know whether he is enjoying the work or not.

Try using Clouded Leopard TTouches around the ears and along the jaw

My dog doesn't like TTouch work around his eyes, head and ears

- Start with the back of your hand or fingers
- Check that you are not pressing or sliding over the skin
- Remember to breathe and keep the movements fluid and relaxed
- Try ear work (opposite)

Working methodically around the head and face can be very relaxing for the dog

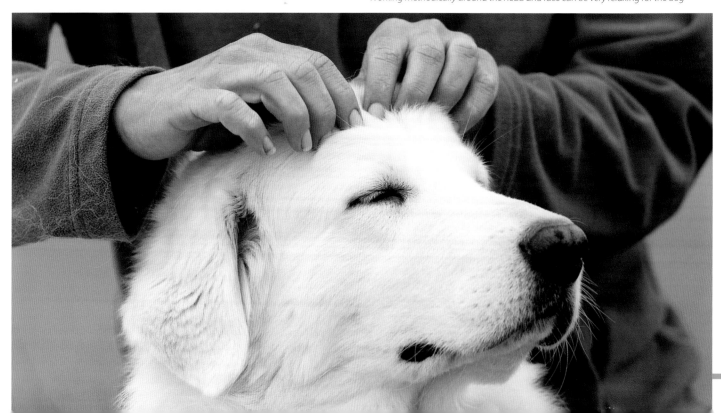

Ear work

Ear work is a really useful tool that every dog owner should learn. As well as helping to release tension around the base of the ears, the forehead, and upper part of the neck, ear work can help dogs overcome a variety of issues and can even save lives. It reduces stress, initiates the parasympathetic nervous system (see p.14), lowers the heart rate and respiration, promotes deep, rhythmical breathing, which boosts the immune system, and can stabilize a dog that is fatigued, stressed or going into or already in a state of shock (see p.35).

Ear work also promotes relaxation and can be done during training and before and after competitions to calm and settle the dog. It can be used during whelping if the bitch becomes distressed and is excellent for helping to warm a cold and exhausted pup. It is also useful for enabling dogs to overcome:

- Ear shyness
- Issues with being handled around the collar
- The effects of cold
- Stiffness
- Nervousness
- Car sickness

If the dog has ears that hang, stroke the ear gently downwards without pulling

- Hyperactivity
- Concerns about treatment for ear problems

- Holding the ear gently but firmly stroke it from the base right out to the tip. If the ear hangs down you will work from the base down, and if the dog has upright ears you will work from the base up to the tip. Move the position of your hand each time to ensure that the whole ear is covered with the strokes. Work gently but with intent. If you are too tentative you may make your dog nervous, particularly if he is ear shy.

- Working the shock point by making circular movements on the tip of the ear with the finger and thumb is beneficial for dogs that have had a traumatic experience, have cold tips to their ears and/or are habitually nervous.

- The speed with which you work will vary on the dog's response and the situation. To calm a nervous or hyperactive dog and to promote relaxation work quite slowly. If your dog is unsure, start by working more quickly initially and then gradually slow the movements as the dog settles. If you are working with a dog that is fatigued, or wanting to help bring a dog round from sedation, work a little more quickly.

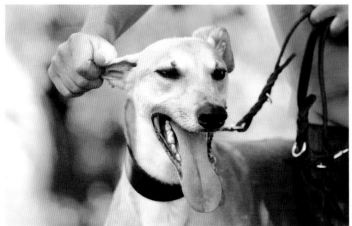

Stroking the ear from the base to the tip is calming and relaxing

My dog doesn't like ear work

- If your dog is concerned try stroking the ear gently against his neck. Some dogs find it more acceptable to have the ear touch their own body initially
- Try covering your hand with a glove or sheepskin mitt (p.126)
- Try holding the ear near the base and very gently take it slightly out to the side, pause for a moment and then slowly guide it back
- Try the other exercises in this section and also exercises for the muzzle and neck (pp.98–101 and 104–105)

THE NECK

TTouches and Python Lifts

Changing the way the dog is led (see pp.82–90) is an important step in helping to reduce tension in the neck. A combination of bodywork and groundwork can also bring dramatic improvements to the way the dog behaves both on and off the lead. As well as using Racoon TTouches (p.97) around the base of the skull and Clouded Leopard TTouches (p.96) on the neck you can also experiment with the Python Lift.

While Python Lifts can be done anywhere on the body, on the neck they can teach a dog to soften and release through the neck which will have a knock-on effect through the back. Python Lifts help to release tight soft tissues and muscle spasms, and increase circulation. In addition they help to:

- Improve movement
- Relax and calm dogs or reduce excitability
- Relieve tension through the head and ears
- Improve focus

- Place the whole hand lightly on the neck with just enough pressure to gently slide (lift) the skin and muscle towards the back of the skull. Pause for several seconds, and then slowly return the skin to the starting point. Move your hand slightly down the neck and repeat the lift. Continue until you reach the withers.

- If the dog is happy, continue along the whole spine.

- Remember to breathe with the movement. If you slide the skin too much or are resting your hand heavily on the dog he will tense or move away.

Flat collars and/or slip leads can create tension in the neck and encourage pulling

Continue gentle Python Lifts down the length of the spine

Python Lifts on the neck help to release tension and teach a dog to soften his topline

My dog doesn't like Python Lifts

- Try shaking your hand before placing it on the dog – this will lighten your contact
- Reduce the movement by doing half a lift
- Vary the speed with which you work
- Check your own posture
- Try the circular TTouches instead

and teaches the dog to be more considered in his responses. In addition this exercise can:

- Calm a nervous or hyperactive dog
- Teach the dog how to approach another dog in a more appropriate way
- Improve the handler's position and balance
- Teach the dog how to listen
- Improve balance, gait and co-ordination

- Place six to eight cones in a line approximately 2m (8ft) apart. The distance will vary depending on the flexibility, co-ordination and size of the dog. Allow enough room between the cones for you and the dog to be able to negotiate them easily without crowding each other. You can narrow the distance between them to encourage greater flexion as you both improve your leash work.

Sally is distracted initially but quickly settles and focuses on Tina as she weaves between the cones (sequence below)

Weaving through cones

Teaching a dog to walk or weave through cones or upturned flowerpots encourages movement through the neck, which will help the dog to release through the whole body.

Dogs that are reactive or quick to arousal are often rigid through the neck. Increasing flexibility in this area can help improve behaviour

My dog doesn't like weaving through cones

- Check your posture and balance
- Try increasing the space between the cones
- Teach him to walk around a single cone
- Put a half body wrap (p.93) on him to improve his spatial awareness

THE FOREQUARTERS

Defining the shoulder

This is a simple exercise that the majority of dogs really enjoy. It helps to release tension in the neck and shoulders and improves movement through the front and hind limbs. In addition, defining the shoulder helps dogs that are:

- Dropped or locked in the withers and back
- Worried by contact around their chest and shoulders
- Uneven in their gait
- Knocking agility jumps with their front feet

- Keep a connection with the dog by holding the lead, supporting the collar or by resting your other hand on his chest.

- Starting at the top of the shoulder trace the slope of the shoulder with your fingers. Avoid digging your fingers into the soft tissue but have enough contact to ensure you do not tickle the dog, which would make him uncomfortable.

- Repeat the same movement behind the shoulder and feel for any areas of tension or places where the dog is concerned about the contact.

- Keep the movement fluid and relaxed and if the dog is happy you can start gently 'walking' your fingers down the front and back of the shoulder blade.

My dog doesn't like defining the shoulder

- Check you are not bracing in your own shoulders and arms
- Experiment with the pressure
- Note whether it is contact on specific areas that make the dog unsettled
- Try putting a half body wrap (p.93) on the dog
- Start working somewhere else that is more acceptable for the dog

Trace the slope of the shoulder with your fingers

Repeat the same movement behind the shoulder blade

Watch the dog for his repsonses. He should relax and enjoy the experience

TTouches around the chest

Working around the chest can have a very calming effect on the dog. You can use the Clouded Leopard TTouch (p.96), Python Lifts (p.104) and also try flattening your hand so that you are now moving the skin in one and a quarter circles with the palm of your hand as well as your fingers. Remember to work slowly and make sure your hand remains soft and relaxed. Your dog should start settling and relaxing. Working either side of the breastbone with Clouded Leopard or Raccoon TTouches is particularly beneficial for dogs that are anxious, timid or distressed. In addition TTouches around the chest are helpful for dogs that are:

- Worried or unsure about contact from a wrap or harness
- Out of balance and pull on their lead
- Distributing their weight unevenly through the front limbs
- Restless

- Sit or stand next to your dog so that you are by his shoulder and his head is facing away from you. Avoid leaning right over him.

- Keep a connection with your other hand and start working gently and slowly around the front of the dog's shoulders and across the chest. Work down the chest and between the front legs.

- You only need to repeat this exercise a couple of times on each shoulder before a difference is noted. If your dog is sensitive to contact in any area, only work where he is comfortable. You should see a change in his responses after a few sessions.

My dog doesn't like TTouches around the chest

- Try changing the pressure or the direction of the circles
- Start by working a little more quickly and then slow the movement down
- Start on the side of his shoulder and move gradually around the front of the chest. If he becomes concerned go back to where he felt more comfortable
- Try putting a half body wrap (p.93) on the dog and work on top of the wrap
- Make sure you aren't bracing or holding your breath

Work around the chest and shoulders with Python Lifts

Rocking the withers

Rocking the withers is a beneficial for releasing tight shoulders and withers. It helps the dog to open up through the chest and ribcage, lengthens the stride and encourages lift through the back and hind limb engagement. This can also be used for:

- Encouraging movement in a dog that has become stuck or gone into freeze (p.18)
- Teaching the dog to transfer his weight from side-to-side
- Encouraging the dog to weight his limbs more evenly

- Place one hand, palm down, over the dog's withers. Keep an even connection through your arm and hand and gently send the withers away from you. Pause for a moment and then slowly bring the withers towards you. Repeat this a few times.

When rocking the withers, note whether one side is freer than the other and pay attention to how your dog reorganizes himself during the exercise

Lift your arms, pause and slowly lower. Exhaling on the lift will help you to stay relaxed and will prevent you from pulling the wrap too high

Lifts with a wrap

Use an Ace wrap (see half body wrap, p.93) for these lifts., which have an extraordinary effect on tight muscles. The movement is minimal but has a profound effect on the way on a dog moves. Lifts also:

- Release a tight neck, elbows and shoulders and relax tired, achy legs
- Calm a restless dog
- Accustom the dog to the balance leash plus (p.89)

- Take the wrap diagonally across the sternum, between the dog's front legs and lift your arms slowly up. Pause, then slowly lower your hands. The release encourages the soft tissue to relax so make the downward movement slightly longer than the lift or pause.

My dog doesn't like rocking the withers

- Cup the withers and just think about asking the dog to move slightly away from you then think about gradually releasing to allow him to move back slowly towards you
- Try defining the shoulder (p.106)
- Walk him over raised poles (p.112) to encourage the withers to lift and release

My dog doesn't like lifts with a wrap

- Use TTouches such as the Abalone TTouch (p.115) on his sternum or do gentle back lifts (p.112) with your hands
- Hold the wrap gently in place without lifting it
- Check you are not pulling the wrap too much – removing all the stretch from it will be uncomfortable for him
- Work through the exercises for the back (p.110) to increase mobility in this area

Front leg circles

Moving a dog's front legs in small clockwise and anti-clockwise circles can help loosen stiff shoulders and release the neck and upper part of the back. It can help increase circulation to the lower limb and paw and is a useful part of a warm up and cool down routine for competition and show dogs. It is also helpful for elderly dogs that stiffen up when lying down. You may find that your dog can circle one leg more easily than the other or is significantly stiffer through one limb. In addition, front leg circles are also helpful for:

- Developing a more even gait
- Encouraging hind limb engagement
- Helping the dog to release his neck and topline
- Improving balance
- Dogs that are reluctant to move or in freeze (p.18)

- Support the front limb without gripping the leg. Circle the limb carefully in both directions. If the dog finds it hard to balance, just do a couple of circles and then put the foot down. Keep the range of movement small – taking the leg as far as it will go will cause bracing and may hurt the dog. Circle the leg over the area where his foot would be if it were still on the ground and ensure that you do not pull the limb out to the side.

- Repeat with the other leg.

Ensure that you circle the leg over the place the paw would be if the foot was on the ground

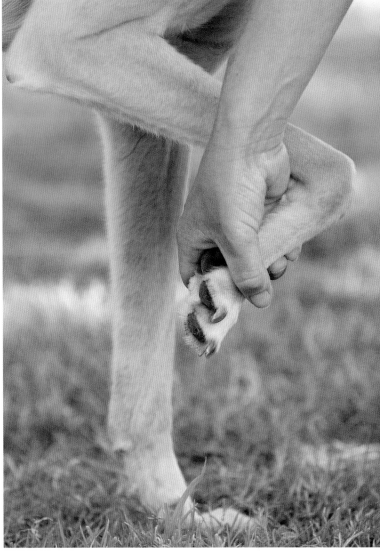

Support the front limb without gripping the leg

My dog doesn't like front leg circles

- Try putting a body half wrap (p.93) on your dog to help him balance
- Use the ground exercises, such as the teeter totter (p.93) and walk-over board (p.93) to improve his balance
- Make sure you are not forcing the circle or pulling the limb
- Watch the movement of the dog as he may have a problem in another limb
- Work through the groundwork exercises including the labyrinth (p.118)
- Rock his withers (opposite)

Uneven poles

When a dog lifts a front leg over a pole, the neck should lower and the withers and shoulders should lift and release. The exception to this is if the dog is tight through the neck, shoulders or back. Walking a dog over uneven poles can help him to release each shoulder alternately. In addition it can be useful for:

• Dogs that are easily distracted and lack focus
• Improving stride length
• Helping to settle reactive or hyperactive dogs

• You can use anything that raises the poles, provided the pole will roll if it is hit. The poles shown here are wooden handrails cut in lengths but you could also use wooden or plastic mop handles, plumbing pipe cut into lengths or lengths of narrow wood. The distance between the poles can be geared to the individual stride of each dog.

THE BACK

TTouch work

Use Clouded Leopard TTouches (p.96) on the back and hindquarters to increase circulation and flexibility. You can also use Raccoon TTouches (p.97) down either side of the spine. The TTouches reduce stress, release tension and its associated behaviour, and connect the dog through his entire body. In addition they are useful for:

• Helping to overcome grooming issues
• Building confidence
• Changing the dog's experience or expectation of hand contact
• Reducing fear and timidity

• You may be more aware of no-go areas on your dog's body when you do TTouches than if you were simply stroking the dog.

• Keep your hand soft, your wrist straight and remember to breathe.

Walking a dog over uneven poles helps him to release through the neck and back

Using TTouches on this little dog has helped to release tension through his lower back

Hair slides

Hair slides (stroking the hair) can have a very relaxing effect. They are useful for introducing contact to an area that may be cause for concern and can help to settle a restless or anxious dog. They can help to reduce overall tension and can quieten a dog that barks or fidgets constantly. In addition hair slides are useful for:

- Dogs that are extremely sensitive to contact
- Helping to overcome issues with grooming
- Releasing tight skin
- Improving the condition of the coat

- Work slowly all over the dog sliding your fingers along and through the hair from the base to the tip. You can start wherever the dog is most comfortable and move gradually towards areas that may be more sensitive.

- If you are working on a smooth-coated dog, imagine that the dog is covered in a light coating of powder and use your fingertips to gently 'pick up' the imaginary powder. Keep the fingers soft and your hand light and vary the speed, particularly if the dog is anxious or unsure.

My dog doesn't like hair slides

- Check that you are not pulling the dog's hair or pinching the skin
- Take less hair and just stroke the tips

Slide your fingers along the hair from the base to the tip

Back lifts

Provided it is safe to handle the dog when he is anxious, back lifts help to soften and release his back, altering his posture, and so his response. They help to open and free the ribs, encourage deep rhythmical breathing and soften and lower the neck. They are also useful for:

• Digestive disturbances and improving health and wellbeing
• Teaching core stability
• Releasing tension through the shoulders and hips

• Squat or stand next to your dog and hold the lead in the hand furthest from him. Place your other hand, palm up, on his sternum and slowly apply a little pressure upwards. Hold this position for a while and then slowly release the movement maintaining the contact with the dog.

• Slide your hand along the sternum and repeat the exercise. The aim is not to lift the dog off his feet but to gently soften and lift the withers and back.

My dog doesn't like back lifts

• Work through the other exercises for the back including raised poles (right)
• Try the belly lifts with the Ace wrap (p.114)
• Place your hand on the sternum and just think about making the movement

Raised poles

This exercise is similar to the uneven poles (p.110). If you plan to incorporate groundwork into your training it is worth investing in some 'polepods'. These are light plastic cups that support the poles and are versatile and easy to transport. You can alter the height and width between the poles to keep your groundwork varied.

Raised poles encourage the dog to lower his neck and to soften and lengthen his topline. They also improve hind limb engagement. In addition they are helpful for:

• Dogs that are reactive to other dogs
• Hyperactive dogs
• Dogs that are tight through their hips and shoulders
• Building core stability
• Improving balance and co-ordination

• Place the poles in a row and gently lead the dog over them.

My dog doesn't like raised poles

• Check that he is not sore in the shoulder, back or hips
• Use Python Lifts (p.104) on his legs and work around his paws
• Start by leading him over a single, flat, narrow length of wood and gradually build up the exercise by adding more lengths of wood
• Make sure that the poles are an appropriate height for the dog's size

Place your hand palm up on the dog's sternum and slowly apply a little pressure upwards

If you are working with a small dog you do not need raised poles – lengths of guttering will work just as well. Note how this little Lowchen softens and releases through the back

THE RIBS, BARREL AND FLANKS

Rib softening

Rib softening increases mobility through the ribs and back and reduces stiffness, helping the dog to be less one-sided. It is useful for:

- Improving balance and turns
- Increasing hind limb function and engagement
- Teaching a dog to soften and yield through the body

- Standing or sitting on the left side of the dog, place your left hand on his left shoulder and your right hand on his opposite hip. Move the right hand slightly towards you while supporting the dog with your other hand. Hold for a moment and then gently release, maintaining a supportive contact on the hip. You should see a very slight flexion through the back and ribs.

- Change your position, place your right hand on the right shoulder and the left hand on the left hip and repeat the exercise. You may find that your dog can soften more easily in one direction than the other. Keep the movement to a minimum and watch your dog's reactions.

Place one hand on the shoulder and the other hand on the opposite hip

My dog doesn't like rib softening

- Do TTouches (pp.95–97) around the shoulders and the hindquarters to accustom him to contact in these areas
- Think of making the movement rather than actually trying to move his hindquarters
- Soften your own shoulders and avoid bracing or tensing
- Try lifts with a wrap (p.114) and back lifts (opposite) with your hands to free the back and ribs
- Lead the dog through the star (p.115) to encourage flexion through the ribs

With the palm of your hand, slowly ask the dog to move his hindquarters towards you. Keep your other hand on the shoulder to support him

Belly lifts and rolls

Belly lifts help dogs to release through the ribs, belly and back. They can relax and settle an anxious dog, and where a dog is picky or off his food can encourage him to eat. In addition they are useful for:

- Encouraging deep breathing and promoting relaxation
- Dogs that freeze (p.18) and hold their breath when nervous
- Digestive disturbances

- Use an Ace wrap (see under half body wrap, p.93) or similar. If your dog is fidgety you may need someone to hold his lead.

- Start the lifts behind the elbows. Holding the ends of the bandage, gently lift for a count of four. Hold for another count of four and then slowly release for a count of eight. The release is the important part of the exercise.

My dog doesn't like belly lifts

- Reduce the lift so that you are barely moving the wrap at all
- Lead the dog over raised poles to start initiating movement in the ribs and spine
- Try the Abalone TTouches (opposite)

Support the ends of the towel or bandage and gently lift one end to create a rolling movement through the skin. Watch the dog for signs of concern

Make contact with the ribs and belly but don't pull the bandage tight

Pause for a moment and then slowly lower while raising the other end. The small blue marker on his back is used to indicate the mobility of Trevor's skin

Abalone TTouches

This is a very warming TTouch that releases tight ribs and tense belly muscles. It is helpful for dogs that are pining, or have digestive problems or those that pant or bark excessively. In addition it helps to:

- Reduce anxiety and promote relaxation
- Settle and calm

- Place the flat of your hand on the dog's sternum and rest your other hand lightly on his back or hold the lead. Move the skin over the sternum in individual circles (see p.96) and move your hand slightly back after each circular movement. Work along the sternum and belly. Watch the dog for his reactions at all times as some dogs are worried by contact on the belly.

Abalone TTouches are very warming and relaxing

My dog doesn't like Abalone TTouches

- Check your posture – bracing will cause the dog to tense
- Make sure you aren't applying pressure by mistake
- Ensure you are moving the skin in a circle rather than simply sliding over the coat, which may tickle the dog
- Work through the exercises to release tension in the back (pp.110–112)

Star

Walking a dog in an arc over a fan – or star – of poles can have a calming effect on him. It also helps to open the ribcage and engage the hindquarters. In addition this exercise is good for:

- Balance and encouraging even turns
- Improving eye/paw co-ordination
- Releasing the shoulders and neck

- Place a minimum of four poles in a fan shape. Raise one end of the poles to make the exercise a little more difficult. Add more poles to create more of an arc or to make a weaving pattern so that the dog changes direction every few strides.

- Start by leading the dog over the lower ends of the poles. Allow him time to pick his way carefully. Do not force him over them if he is nervous.

- Lead him in both directions. If he is happy walking over the lower ends, ask him to walk over the middle of the poles to encourage him to lift his legs higher.

Walking a dog over the star helps to increase flexibility through the ribs and improves paw/eye co-ordination

My dog doesn't like the star

- Try using straight poles
- Teach the dog to move in an 'S' or shallow serpentine without the poles
- Check your position – if you are too far back or are pulling on the lead the dog will be thrown off balance

THE HINDQUARTERS AND TAIL

Python Lifts

A high proportion of dogs are nervous about being handled around the hindquarters. Start by using the Python Lifts (p.104) on the back and move your hand slowly down to the pelvis and tail. You can then work down the down hind limbs.

- Start on the hip and lift the skin in an upwards direction for a moment with the palm of your hand, pause for a moment and then guide the skin slowly back down. Move your hand slightly lower and repeat the movement curling your fingers gently around the leg as you work downwards.

Move your hand slowly down the hind limb, making Python Lifts as you go

If your dog is calm, continue making Python Lifts down the leg to the foot curling your fingers gently around the limb as you work

Hind leg circles

Moving a dog's hind legs in small clockwise and anti-clockwise circles can help loosen stiff hindquarters. It also enables a dog to release through the back and can increase circulation to the limbs. This is a quick and easy way of helping elderly dogs that stiffen up during the colder weather. You may find that the dog can circle one leg more easily than other, is reluctant to pick up one leg or is significantly stiffer on one side. Dogs that are dropped in the pelvis will have reduced mobility in the corresponding leg.

- Pick up the leg nearest you and circle it slowly over the place the foot would be if it were still on the ground and the dog was standing square. Keep the range of movement small and avoid pulling the limb out to the side.

Support the hind leg and circle the foot carefully over the area the paw would be if the foot was still on the ground

My dog doesn't like hind leg circles

- Start with the front limbs (p.109)
- Try tail work (below) first
- Put your hand on the hips and rock the dog slowly from side to side to teach him how to transfer his weight from side to side. This is similar to rocking the withers (p.108), but works on the pelvis

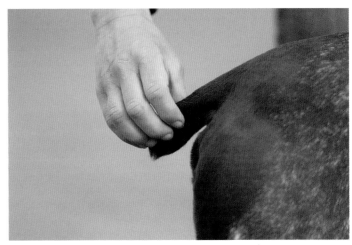

You can use Clouded Leopard TTouches on either side of the dog's tail. Docked dogs particularly benefit from tail work

Tail work

A busy tail is often accompanied by a busy mouth. Tail work can help a dog to become less vocal and to release tight back muscles. It can also reduce tension in the back and hindquarters. It enables the dog to move beyond instinctive flight/fight responses (see p.18) and can improve movement through the hips, which allows dogs to jump more easily into a car or walk upstairs. As a non-habitual movement, tail work gives the dog's nervous system a new experience and encourages him to relax through the entire body. It improves the connection from the head to the end of the tailbone and can reduce frantic or hyperactive behaviours. In addition tail work can be useful for:

- Dogs that are nervous, timid and/or noise-sensitive
- Dogs that lack engagement
- Dogs that weight one hind limb more than the other
- Improving articulation through the hocks
- Achieving or maintaining a sit and stay

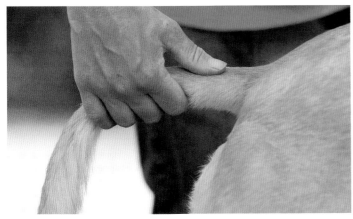

Support the tail lightly with one hand and circle the tail gently in both directions

- Circle the tail gently in both directions. As you make the circles, think of the movement coming through your body and shoulders rather than just your arms. Softening your knees will keep the movement relaxed. The size of the circles depends on the tightness of the tail. Always keep them within a range of motion that is comfortable for the dog. If the tail is clamped, place your hand over top of the tail and make a circular movement with your hand.

- There are several ways that you can use the TTouches on the tail: If your dog is nervous about being handled around the tail, cup your hand over the top of the tail and use the Python Lifts (opposite) down the tail and hind legs. Taking the body more into its habitual posture is often an effective way of releasing tension. You can also try gently rocking the dog from side-to-side with your hand supporting the upper tail and hindquarters.

  If your dog is happy to be handled around the tail, try using the circular TTouches down either side of the tailbone feeling and looking for areas where there may be reduced mobility or areas that cause concern for the dog. Tail issues are often linked to tension in the back.

If your dog is nervous about being handled around the tail, cup your hand over the top of the tail and use Python Lifts down the tail and hind legs

- Tail work can be unsettling for some dogs and you may need to build up slowly to handling him around the hindquarters and tail.

Labyrinth

The labyrinth can be used to improve co-ordination and to increase body awareness. It is excellent for dogs that may be on restricted exercise and is a wonderful tool for helping dogs to connect to their hindquarters. It has a calming effect on most dogs and encourages efficient brain/body use. In addition it is good for:

- Improving balance
- Nervous or hyperactive dogs
- Dogs recovering from cruciate ligament problems (this should, of course, be checked with your vet)
- Improving self-control

- Set up the labyrinth as shown in the photo below, using poles, lengths of wood or guttering. Lead the dog slowly through it.

My dog doesn't like the labyrinth

- Use TTouches on his hindquarters
- Try putting a half body wrap (p.93) on him
- Start by leading him past a single pole on the ground, then between two poles, gradually building up the exercise

This little Lowchen is over the top in his responses to people

The labyrinth has a very calming effect. Lead the dog slowly through it, ensuring the turns are not too tight

THE FEET

Foot work

Sensitive feet can cause problems for both dogs and owners alike. Helping your dog to overcome his concerns makes life easier when it comes to treating a split pad, cleaning muddy paws or trimming nails. In addition work around the feet can be useful for:

- Nervous dogs
- Improving an irregular gait
- Overly sensitive dogs
- Dogs that are worried by noise or travelling in the car

There are several ways that you can help to teach a dog to accept contact on his feet.

- Use a horse schooling stick or soft paintbrush to stroke the leg and paws if the dog is worried by contact from your hand. If he is likely to nip, start with the schooling stick and avoid leaning over him. Make sure that the contact is firm without being too hard. A light touch will tickle the dog and unsettle him more.

Below left: If the dog is settling, use Raccoon TTouches around his toes and nails
Below right: If he is still worried, circle the paw on the opposite leg
Bottom left: Progress to working on the pads and upper part of the paw
Bottom right: You can also use tiny TTouches on either side of his nails

If your dog is nervous about being handled on the paws start by using a stick to stroke him down the chest and front limbs

- If the dog is happy, progress to a fake hand (p.31) or a stuffed glove attached to a stick. If he is still happy, use the back of your hand to make light, flicking movements down the limbs to the feet. Working quickly may be more tolerable.

- If the dog is settling, do Raccoon TTouches (p.97) around his toes, down either side of his nails and finally on his pads. If he becomes concerned go back to an area that was acceptable. If he is still unsure, lift a front leg and use the paw to make circular movements on the opposite leg (see photograph, near left). It can be more acceptable at first for the dog to feel his own body against his foot.

My dog doesn't like foot work

- Break it down into several sessions over several weeks if necessary
- Work little and often
- Practise the exercises to release the shoulders (pp.106–110) and hips (pp.116–118)
- Try not to set a goal or fixate on overcoming the problem
- Stay calm and relaxed
- Walk him over different surfaces (p.120)

Different surfaces

Some dogs panic when they have to walk across a slippery surface or on something that moves beneath their feet, such as the seat of a car. Walking over different surfaces enables them to become more confident and more focused. This exercise also improves sensory integration, balance and proprioception. In addition it helps to:

- Encourage the dog to think
- Quieten exuberant or over the top behaviours
- Stimulate the brain

- A variety of surfaces can be used including a bath mat, car mat, door mat, dog bed, plastic sheeting, wooden board, blanket or carpet. You can also obtain some cheap plastic trays and fill them with different materials such as sand, water, earth or gravel. Lay them out in any pattern and walk the dog slowly over them.

My dog doesn't like different surfaces

- Make the steps simple and work with one surface at a time
- Increase core strength and stability by using the exercises for the back (pp.110–112) and ribs, barrel and flanks (pp.113–115)
- Try leg circles (p.109 and 116) and stroke the legs with a horse schooling stick to help bring awareness to the feet

If the dog can sit on the surface it is an indication that he feels safe and is not worried by the sensation under his feet

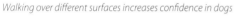

Walking over different surfaces increases confidence in dogs

Allow him to explore the surface with his nose

Pick up sticks/ladder

Teaching a dog to negotiate his way over obstacles can improve eye/paw co-ordination. This is useful for developing balance and can help to teach an agility dog more awareness of foot placement. In addition these exercises:

- Help dogs that stumble and trip
- Improve confidence
- Aid concentration and thoughtful action
- Slow down dogs that rush and pull

- Lay a minimum of six poles in any pattern on the ground varying the angles and spacing between each pole and/or use an old wooden ladder.

- Ask the dog to walk forward carefully over the obstacles. Even the bounciest dog can learn to become lighter on his feet and more precise with his paws.

My dog doesn't like pick up sticks/ladder

- Stroke his legs with a horse schooling stick (p.119)
- Teach him to walk over a single pole and gradually add more
- Try a half body wrap (p.93) or face elastic (p.100) to improve focus and balance
- Walk him over different surfaces (opposite)

Ollie is easily distracted and pulls when on the lead. He struggles with the exercise at first

Ollie lacks self-control , which is why he finds this exercise challenging. He begins to lower his head and concentrate, gradually becoming more focused and co-ordinated

Working over ladders and poles improves paw/eye co-ordination

HOLISTIC DOG CARE

By being aware of how dogs respond and react to the environment that we create for them, we can enhance their day-to-day existence and enjoy a long and loyal partnership, based on understanding, co-operation and trust.

Know the whole dog

Incorporating some of the TTouches into your everyday handling of your dog will help to keep him calm, supple and content, and will alert you to even the smallest of changes in his physical, mental and emotional wellbeing, as soon as they occur. Even if you don't have the time to work through every groundwork exercise in this book, a few of them, done a couple of times a week will improve his confidence, movement and co-ordination. Sometimes a single session may be all it takes before you see a difference in your dog.

By understanding your dog on a whole new level you can start to plan a strategy that fits into your schedule and that will help him to overcome any worries he may have. There are usually threads linking unwanted behaviours and areas of tension. Observe the way these threads weave together and you will see the bigger picture.

Exercise

It is not vital that you walk your dog every single day. While exercise is, of course, extremely important, it can be detrimental in the cases

Emergency measures

If your dog becomes over-aroused when out and about, walk him through an imaginary labyrinth in the park or walk him in an S-shape and use the TTouches to help him settle. Put a T-shirt, dog coat or half body wrap (p.93) on him and see if he is calmer when he has sensory input from the article.

By understanding our dogs on a whole new level, we can enrich their lives, and ours

Watch your dog's reactions to your voice

of some timid or over the top dogs, which become more agitated with increased exposure to stimuli. Other dogs may be on reduced exercise due to age, injury or ill health. In these cases keep outside exercise to a minimum until your dog grows in confidence or regains full health and in the meantime work through some of the groundwork exercises in the book to improve his levels of confidence or to increase mobility. They will help to keep your dog physically and mentally stimulated without overloading him.

In addition, work on your own balance and try to become more aware of your habitual behaviours and responses. Watch your dog's reactions to your voice, body language and movement as you go about your daily routine.

Some timid or over the top dogs become more agitated when they are outside

Sometimes a single session is all it takes to help a dog grow in confidence

Equipment

You do not need to invest vast amounts of money in purchasing groundwork equipment. Be inventive. Use car mats, wooden boards, bath mats, carpet offcuts, towels, old dog blankets and so on to create different surfaces; old broom handles, lengths of old plastic plumbing pipe or guttering are ideal for polework. You can even use old lengths of rope to lay out a labyrinth and flowerpots, old buckets or plastic bottles filled with sand for weave cones. You are limited only by your own imagination.

If your dog is on reduced exercise, use groundwork to improve his co-ordination and confidence

TTouch can be enjoyed by the whole family

Emergency harness

In an emergency, you can use a length of soft rope to make a harness quickly. This type of harness is useful if a dog needs to be controlled effectively, but kindly, such as at the vet's clinic. The advantage of making this harness is you don't need to put it over the dog's head or lift his front legs as with a traditional harness – so your actions won't be seen as invasive or threatening by a dog you don't know – and it can be easily removed. Used with a lead attached to the collar, the harness reduces pulling on the neck if the dog is recovering from surgery or is highly stressed.

Hold the loop snugly over the withers with one hand and make a loop in the two lengths of rope. Push it through the knotted loop

Take a 6m (20ft) length of rope and tie a small loop in the middle of it

Pass one end of the rope around the dog's chest

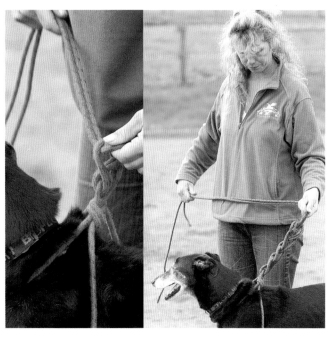

Braid more loops and finish off the harness by taking the tails of the rope through your final loop. This will keep it all together

Throw the other end of the rope under the dog's ribs towards you – this is safer than passing it under the ribs from your side, which means you have to lean over the dog to pick it up on the other side

To release the harness – take the tails out of the final loop and gently pull on them. The whole harness should unravel easily and fall to the floor

House training

If you are struggling to house train your dog and have used all the right positive training techniques there are a few other things to consider. Some dogs are nervous about going out in the dark because their vision is poor. This doesn't just occur in older dogs but can be a problem from birth. Some dogs are worried about squatting in a vulnerable position outside, particularly if they are sore or tight in the pelvis and hips and/or if they live with a very boisterous canine companion. They may play in the garden and then rush back inside to relieve themselves much to the frustration of their owners. Others may be agoraphobic because they are noise-sensitive or worried by a dog (or cat!) next door, or may have a medical problem that requires veterinary attention.

If you suspect any of these, you can also use the TTouches to help your dog grow in confidence. Avoid punishing him if he makes a mess in the house. If he is shouted at or smacked, he will become more insecure and the problem will escalate.

Patting and grooming

If you pat your dog note how hard you pat, particularly if the dog is young, old, uncomfortable, shy or easily aroused. Watch his responses and see if he truly enjoys the experience or braces and politely waits for you to stop. Try keeping your hand soft and light next time you pat him or better still, use TTouches to praise him or to connect with him. Use gentle ear work (p.103) instead of ruffling him around the head, which can be extremely stimulating to an already excitable dog.

Grooming should not be a chore nor uncomfortable for the dog. It is a way of relaxing him and ensuring that his coat and skin remain healthy. Regular grooming enables you to carry out health checks and look for small nicks, bites or sores.

Start with a sheepskin mitt if your dog has any concerns about being touched or groomed on any part of his body

A soft rubber groomer is invaluable for a dog that is nervous about being brushed

Groom him with a sheepskin mitt or soft rubber grooming tool if he is worried by brushes and combs, and work slowly and calmly in short sessions if necessary. Use hair slides (p.111) and light TTouches to increase circulation, to improve a dull or lifeless coat and to release tight skin that may make grooming uncomfortable.

Bedtime

Watch to see whether your dog is truly happy to go to his bed or whether he only goes on a command or at night. If necessary, move his bed so that he feels confident to rest there during the day. Some dogs, especially those that are noise-sensitive, may be unwilling to sleep in a particular spot such as next to a boiler or washing machine if there is a choice to be some place quieter instead.

Make sure his bed is actually comfortable and of an appropriate size and shape for him. Some dogs like to stretch out while asleep, while others prefer to curl up. Some dogs like a hard bed and others a soft one.

Cleaning products

Beware of using toxic products to clean utility rooms/and or kitchen floors and sinks. Some dogs increase their manic behaviours if products containing bleach are used in their environment. Others may have allergic responses to everyday household products.

Diet

We are what we eat and the same applies for our dogs. Although some people dispute that there is a link between unwanted behaviour and an inappropriate diet, the two often walk hand-in-hand. Not every dog will do well on the same food, and different breeds have different needs. Consult a holistic veterinarian who specializes in nutrition if your dog experiences ongoing problems.

Above all, enjoy learning more about your dog and remember that you already have the tools you need to help him: your eyes and your hands and your desire to make a difference to your companion's life.

Useful Addresses and Further Reading

TTouch Addresses
Sarah Fisher
TTouch UK
Tilley Farm
Farmborough
Bath BA2 0AB
Tel. 01761 471182
www.ttouchteam.co.uk
sarahfisher@ttouch.co.uk

Robyn Hood
TTouch Canada
5435 Rochdell Road
Vernon BCV1B 3E8
Canada
www.tteam-ttouch.ca

Linda Tellington Jones
TTouch USA
PO Box 3793
Santa Fe
New Mexico 87501
USA
www.ttouch.com

TTouch South Africa
www.ttouchsa.co.za

Other Useful Addresses
Association of Chartered Physiotherapists in Animal Therapy (ACPAT)
www.acpat.org

Association of Pet Dog Trainers (APDT)
www.apdt.co.uk
www.apdt.com

Association of Pet Behaviour Counsellors (APBC)
www.apbc.org.uk

Sarah Heath BVSc MRCVS
Behavioural Referrals Veterinary Practice
11 Cotebrook Drive
Upton
Chester CH2 1RA
England
Tel. 01244 377365
Fax. 01244 399228
admin@vetethol.demon.co.uk

Sound Therapy 4 Pets Ltd
Sounds Scary
(for treatment of dogs that have got sound phobias)
Sounds Sociable
(for puppy habituation to a wide range of sounds)
Sounds Soothing
(for preparing dogs for living with children and babies)
www.soundtherapy4pets.com
UK Tel. 01244 371473

Veterinary Products Laboratories (VPL)
301 W. Osborn Rd.
Phoenix AZ 85013 USA
Tel. 888-241-9545
(Customer Service)
www.vpl.com

McTimoney Chiropractic Association
www.mctimoney-chiropractic.org

Robin Walker BVetMed MRCVS
contactable via the APBC (left)

Nick Thompson BSc (Hons), BVMBS, VetMFHom, MRCVS
Holistic Vet Ltd,
Weston Chiropractic Clinic
Apthorp
Weston Road
Bath BA1 2XT
England
www.holisticvet.co.uk

Marie Miller
61 Grange Road
Longford
Coventry
West Midlands CV6 6DB
England
Tel. 02476 366090
www.pawsnlearn.com
ttouch@pawsnlearn.com

Maria Johnston
13 Spa Lane
Hinckley
Leicester LE10 1JA
England
Tel. 01455 457350

Kendal Shepherd BVSc MRCVS CCAB
16 Church Street
Finedon
Wellingborough
Northamptonshire NN9 5NA,
England
kendal@lindenarts.co.uk
Tel. 01933 681640

Acupressure for Dogs
Amy Snow and Nancy Zidonis
Tallgrass Animal Acupressure
4559 Red Rock Drive
Larkspur CO 80118
USA
www.animalacupressure.com

Karen Pryor Clicker Training
www.clickertraining.com

Books, Videos and CDs
Getting in TTouch with Your Dog
Linda Tellington Jones
ISBN: 1-872119-41-7

Unleash Your Dog's Potential – Getting in TTouch with your dog video with Linda Tellington Jones
ISBN: 1-872119-44-i

Haynes Dog Training Manual
Carolyn Menteith
ISBN: 1-844253-51-1

The Well Connected Dog
Amy Snow and Nancy Zidonis
ISBN 0-9645982-4-8

Four Paws Five Directions
Cheryl Schwartz DVM
ISBN: 780890 877906

Clicker Training for Dogs
Karen Pryor
ISBN: 1-86054-282-4

Blue Dog Interactive CD
particularly good for teaching children about dogs. Available from www.thebluedog.org

The Canine Commandments
Kendal Shepherd BVSc, CCAB, MRCVS
ISBN: 978-1-874092-55-1

Acknowledgments

Thanks to Bob Atkins, Tina Constance, Robyn Hood, Kerry Jenkinson, Maria Johnston, Marie Miller, Kaye Mughal and all the staff and dogs at Battersea Old Windsor and Battersea Cats and Dogs Home, Adam Rogers, Amy Snow, Linda Tellington Jones, Nick Thomson, and, of course, Jo Weeks my fabulous editor!

The quotation used in the foreword and on page 75 is paraphrased from the words of American physician and writer Oliver Wendell Holmes (1809–94):
'A mind once expanded by a new idea,
Never returns to its original dimensions.'